# The 7th Seal

### Hidden Wisdom Unveiled

*A Reflection of Self-Discovery*

*Revised & Expanded*

VOL. 1

*By Mathues Imhotep*

*"Know what is in front of your eyes and what is hidden will be disclosed to you, for there is nothing hidden that will not be revealed."* ~ Gospel of Thomas (Gnostic Scriptures)

Copyright © 1997-2004 by Mathues Imhotep

ALL RIGHTS RESERVED. NO PART OF THIS DOCUMENT MAY BE REPRODUCED OR TRANSMITTED IN ANY FORM OR BY ANY MEANS, ELECTRONIC OR MECHANICAL, INCLUDING PHOTOCOPYING, RECORDING, OR BY ANY INFORMATION STORAGE AND RETRIEVAL SYSTEM.

## TABLE OF CONTENTS

Desiring the Light.................................................................13

Story of 'In the Beginning'....................................................17

Balance is the Key...............................................................19

The Grand Shift...................................................................22

Ascension is the Way............................................................25

Pistis Sophia.......................................................................28

The Corner Stone in Phi........................................................30

Seeds of Life......................................................................33

Foundation of the Tree of Life...............................................38

Cosmology of the Creator.....................................................40

The Fruit of Life.................................................................43

Was he a she?....................................................................45

144 Children of Light...........................................................51

Creation of Life..................................................................53

Creational Flow - The Divine Unfolding...................................55

Eve gives life to Adam.........................................................60

The Early Church Fathers......................................................64

Remember, Behold Seth's Great Race......................................72

Cosmology of the Geometric Twinships....................................77

Melchizedek Dispensation ....................................................81

Mystery Schools..................................................................86

Egyptian Initiation...............................................................90

Kings Resurrected...............................................................92

Ascension Tools..................................................................97

Osiris's Backbone..............................................................105

Serapis the Gnostic Egyptian...............................................107

The Divine Ratio of Proportions............................................115

The Sacred Cut..................................................................119

Golden Spirals of Life.........................................................121

Phi Snake........................................................................128

Entrance into Knowledge of All Existing Things........................130

Seeing Phi........................................................................135

Sacredness of Five.............................................................138

The Esoteric Spirit of Five...................................................143

"Phi-ve" sided Magic..........................................................148

The PHI of Life .................................................................153

3-4-5 PHI-Angle................................................................154

Egyptian Proportions..........................................................159

Mystery in Egypt.................................................................................................163

Gnostic Mystery..................................................................................................165

The 24 Disciples.................................................................................................171

Bridal Chamber - A Great Mystery Revealed................................................175

"Wheel within Wheels"......................................................................................179

Bridal Chamber Ceremony Recital..................................................................181

First Wavers........................................................................................................191

Twin Flames Reunite........................................................................................194

The End to this Eternal Story..........................................................................201

Lonely for Love...................................................................................................203

Three Key principles for the Dimensional Shift............................................205

Seven powerful keys to the "Inner Door".......................................................208

The Energy Retrieval Process ..........................................................................211

Matrix of Polarities..........................................................................................212

Afterword............................................................................................................214

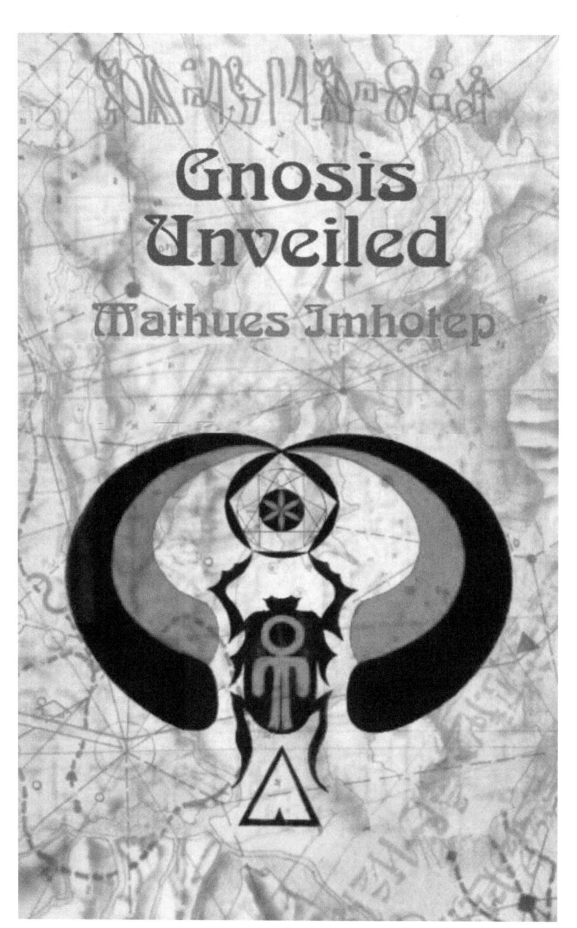

*Golden Gate*
*Ascension of Consciousness into Divine Intelligence*

# Preface

This book wrote itself, and, in the process, it wrote, confirmed and defined me. The writing process was an inner journey that most conclusively proved to me the existence of an unseen hand that is definitely weaving a greater tapestry of unity and interconnectedness among humanity. This book is designed to reveal many things by encouraging a discovery of yourself and the underlying truths of reality.

I would like to provide some background information that I feel is necessary to understand that which will be put forth here as a new foundational spiritual framework. In many ways the contents of this book are not new at all, but very ancient. To many, the tenets presented may seem very new and widely divergent from what has been the norm or the pontificated belief systems of academia and the world religions. Some people, on the other hand, will innately recognize the words as truth, for they will absolutely ring or resonate in their hearts; for indeed, we all have the encoding of universal truths embedded in our core, from the microscopic level of our cells to the macro-cosmic ethers of our spiritual body or souls.

What has guided me from the beginning is an inner knowing, the "still small voice" that we can hear if only we will stop long enough to listen. In many cases, on my own spiritual path to self-realization and enlightenment, there has been a strong presence, an almost overt influence, which I just could not ignore. My passion for life, love and truth has continuously beckoned me to my highest path and when I would falter, as we all do, that all-knowing guiding hand would gently encourage my continued path of seeking the narrow way and high road. I would be remiss not to mention that, in some cases that hand has had the need to be somewhat stern and strong, giving me a loving push.

This is the first of three books in this series: Gnosis Unveiled. I have known for over five years that I would be writing several books. My guidance has finally indicated that now is the time. With the events that have transpired recently, the culmination of a life-long understanding has been verified and confirmed beyond my wildest dreams. My whole life's purpose has ultimately been revealed through the chain of events that have resulted in the near total recall of my soul's akashic history as a leader of spiritual reconstitution.

I have always known several principal maxims about the nature of existence, which have served as the backbone of my spiritual valor. These firm and sound spiritual cornerstones have been the rock that my faith has been built upon. In this book I will divulge five elements laying the groundwork for our personal sacred temple, as we proceed into the greater mysteries that have been revealed, remembered and channeled through and by me (and my higher self.) Additionally, these five elements represent the five initiations that initiates would undergo in the ancient mystery schools.

The release of this information coincided with several other major events that have to do with the greatest of personal paradigm shifts. For several decades now, there has truly been a significant undercurrent carrying and directing the consciousness of humankind. The time is fast approaching when this seemingly unnoticed tributary will gather with the greater river of awakening consciousness and plummet into the ocean of full realization as a vast divine awareness.

For now is most definitely a paramount time, indeed, with many predictions and utterances of "End Times" and redeeming raptures. These millennium end-days are without question the most anticipated pivotal period of hundreds, if not thousands of years. The warnings are many, and, unfortunately, they far outweigh any favorable predictions that have come forth. Again, my responsibility, (though certainly not solely mine, but rather a responsibility being accepted by many now) is to be a harbinger of the new "Golden Age." With every new age, there must be the conclusion of the preceding one. However, let us not lose sight of the future that such ending brings. For what has become clear to me through this work is that the preponderance of information, both prophetic and speculative, concerning the breaking of the purported seventh seal of the Bible's Revelation is not, as many would or have you believe, a great judgment of doom and gloom for the sinners. Instead, and perhaps surprisingly for some, it is a time when by choice the "dead (metaphoric sleeping) will come out of their graves," resounding in resurrection of consciousness and the co-creation of a new Golden Age, at last fulfilling those prophecies which have remained untainted through the ages, as we shall gladly see.

In the innermost circles of the metaphysical esoteric cadre, there exists a belief - - a deeply cherished vision. This reverie of unseen messengers has called to subtly inclined minds for quite some time, heralding the foretold Promised Land, a heaven on Earth. These divinely inspired inner glances have been called by such names as: dimensional shift, enlightenment, self-realization and ascension. Great is the covenant of peace and utopia pledged, lying just beyond the millennium's first ledge, a mere decade of uncharted waters, with only minor fears to tread: 2012 is a consciousness odyssey in the not too distant future.

[Author's notes in 2017 during my revised editing in preparation for releasing more hidden wisdom, as I received things that I was not allowed to release until the 6th Seal had been broken. This occurred in 2014 when Easter happened at the same time all around the world and the grand fixed cross occurred in the sky during an Eclipse and Blood moon. This was the beginning of the Blood Moon Ally that resulted in 7 major blood moons. When I first began to write this book, I was definitely seeing the future, as I gazed into the center of my being and saw a time in the future well past 2012 (I began the notes that comprised the material to start this book in 1996), when there was a specific moment that represented the grand awakening of humankind (rather than Mankind.) This time was the actual unveiling of the 7th Seal itself. This would be akin to what the Book of Revelations is talking about to a degree. As we shall see! I have also used this phrase many times in this book because I knew all this would come to pass and that the building up of this material and understanding would lead to a destination that was incredible! Over the decades since I first started writing this series, I have been shown many things, on many levels. Including the behind the scenes of the Chinese Elders, New Financial Systems and a Currency Revaluation on a Global scale. I will release more of this hidden history of my past decade working at the highest levels of this secret world of finance in my workshops, videos and radio programs. For now, suffice it to say, I was in for a wild ride when I undertook this journey of Self-Discovery! I will be inserting pertinent comments throughout this revision, as I now know exactly where this journey ends and the meaning of the milestones along the way!]

Whether or not you believe in reincarnation or the eternal conscious existence of the soul, the end is always just a beginning; for regardless of the perceived reality, there always exists the potential for greater accomplishment and understanding. It does not matter for one moment whether reality is of a material nature or not. Existence is existence, a conscious awareness regardless of form. Therefore, as long as you have this current material form and are free to let your mind roam, you may as well pause and open your heart to the greatest, oldest accomplishment potential yet, Resurrection and Ascension. However, this transformation did not actually occur in the manner portrayed in the Bible. It is rather, and more interestingly, a greater mystery. For Jesus says in the Gnostic Scriptures, "Whoever drinks from my mouth will become like me. I myself shall become that person, and the hidden things will be revealed." With an understanding of these words, we will retrace and prove that the mystery schools taught this arcane wisdom of Ascension. Even more specifically, that "God's Wisdom in a mystery, even the wisdom that hath been hidden" was orally taught as the Secret Doctrine which promised "to complete you in the Mysteries of the Kingdom of Light" by those who were initiated "to make the lower like the upper and the outer like the inner, and join them through a Mystery". Finally, "If you know the truth, the truth shall set you free." Also, it has been said: "If we become acquainted with the truth, we shall find the fruits of truth are within us and if we join with it, it will receive our fullness."

All this wisdom can be experienced through what is revealed here as the veracity of a conscious ascension in awakened awareness as the complete, conscious transformation from one reality dimension existence to another, in a wide-awake fashion, without even leaving the farm. (Lighthearted humor is one of the key ingredients to this sacred ancient alchemical formula, thank Goodness.) One of my innate ultimate goals has been and always will be to master this third-dimensional existence of matter, in hopes of simply sharing with others how to transcend the believed limitations of death and gain an eternal awareness of the "I AM." In this heightened state of Gnosis (meaning knowledge or acquaintance by a personal experience or connection to the Creator), "The End" simply does not exist, as conscious life is truly an eternal state. In this newly perceived reality, we will learn that we are the quintessential co-creators of our infinite reality experiment.

*"The moment of truth, the sudden emergence of a new insight, is an act of intuition. Such intuitions give the appearance of miraculous flashes, or short-circuits of reasoning. In fact they may be likened to an immersed chain, of which only the beginning and the end are visible above the surface of consciousness. The diver vanishes at one end of the chain and comes up at the other, guided by invisible links."* — Arthur Koestler[1]

I welcome you to embark on a journey of self-discovery, a reclaiming of your original divine heritage and birthright, not to be missed. May your own heart and inner knowing recognize and resonate with the golden threads of truth that have been sewn together here in a most amazing tapestry of ubiquitous unity by an undeniable presence --- the all-pervasive invisible hand. I have come to accept my job as a messenger, and in so doing, I place these words of wisdom at your feet for your own heart's discernment. This is done in the hope that your soul will resound in delight at its own recognition of its passionate part in this long road of torch totting, as one of the many "Keepers of Truth". Read this material with an open mind and heart and allow the frequency of light, which has been transmitted from beyond (and within), literally from a place of pure soul and eternal consciousness, to awaken your own soul's blueprint for conscious ascension. This being a greater awareness and understanding of the Creator's many mansions and your part in it. May you too find renewed conviction and greater understanding of our collective journey and feel the presence of the invisible ONE beckoning us on to perfection in complete balance, which enlightens your life and enlivens your step, with a strengthened and spiritually enhanced hope and faith of harmony, joy and eternal freedom. This message is given and delivered throughout this book for the pure sake of Unconditional Love and an unending desire to serve the greater expression of all parts of the whole.

A note to the reader: This work is set up with a sub-title division or topic demarcation to assist the reader in more easily discerning the categorization of the overall material. And in this way several threads of understanding can be delivered.

**Story Line** – The Story Line is my experience as the unfolding plot of what I have witnessed in my life regarding what is being presented here. The following symbol will represent this type of story arch.

**Neo-History** – Neo-History is essentially a retelling or recounting of history with a new precept and look into the old stories, fabled folklore and ancient myths. With a unique symbol for each that follows I will use these symbols to highlight important areas or content.

---

[1]

**Sacred Geometry** – Sacred Geometry is the greater aspect of this work that will represent the logical or left-brain approach to understanding the underpinning natural order of creation

**Gnosis** – Gnosis is the wisdom that is to be gleaned from the amalgamation of the entirety of this work.

**Wisdom** – *Wisdom is the guiding light of the Author's further interjections from an overview understanding, as an Invisible guiding hand that weaves the greater tapestry of insight into the overall story and dissertation. This is also called Achamoth by the Gnostics.*

**Ancient Text** – *Ancient text is the Secret Sayings and Hidden Wisdom of forgotten scriptures revealing the underlying truths of the universe and our place in it.*

**[Author Notes and Key insights]** - **in this Revised Edition I am highlighting key points that I have confirmed or come to understand in a more complete or profound way. There are so many things that I now can reveal or accentuate given everything I have experience or have come to know as absolute.**

As the underlying fabric of this story is the synchronicity of the invisible hands orchestration it becomes important to state as one further preface to beginning this book that it was written approximately three months after I returned from my first trip to Egypt, which was September 24th 1997. Part one of this book was completed in one month, as I most intensely was remembering my part in the mystery schools. This portion of the book is what I term Course 101 on Sacred Geometry and its history, coupled with some of my experiences and beliefs. This section is essentially the lesser mysteries. The second part of the book was written upon my return from Egypt for the second time (November 22nd, 1998), and is primarily the story about the "Opening of the Way" into the mystery school and the greater comprehension of a mandala of interconnected sacred geometry and numerology (Neo-Numerology) as a mirror reflection of the nature of creation and our intimate unity with it. The second portion, effectively name the Greater Mysteries, was written over approximately four months and was prompted by the near-death initiation that I received during my three-month stay in the hospital. I suffered from a strange life-threatening syndrome called Gillian Barre, which causes the immune system to turn against the nervous system, thus paralyzing the body for the duration of treatment and recovery. This syndrome (experienced by 1 out of every 100,000 persons), which left me next to lifeless, in the most unimaginable, unbearable state of complete surrender to pain, which afflicted me on March 17th, 1999. I walked out of physical therapy nearly three months later, on June 5th, a hundred percent detached from my own personal agenda about any perceivable thing at all. In most cases, this disease causes the patient to remain in the hospital for 4-6 months, with an additional 1-5 years for full recovery. Five years later, my feet are still suffering from slight paralysis and pain (approx. 97% recovered).

My earlier life experiences had filled my heart with an extreme passion for life and truth, exciting me to no end with the possibilities. I thought for sure I was previously surrendered and ready to serve, but now I understand what it means to be utterly selfless and detached, even from my own dharma (life's purpose). Being completely empty, free from forcing, making or trying to use my acquired Wisdom to figure out what everything meant or needs to be. I AM truly ready to serve the will of the ONE.

During my post hospital recovery period, unable to work for three years, I carried a deeply renewed selfless torch of inspiration for continuing to complete this most important work as received a very realistic resurrection to life and breath. I finished the second part on November 22nd, 1999. The significance of this date will become obvious and most profound concerning all the divine synchronicities that have orchestrated my entire life. I have always felt that I am a canvas and Spirit the brush that paints me, for create me masterfully or simply abstract, but create me, nonetheless, for I am yours to creatively express the truth through my body canvas.

Have you ever heard the phrase, "watch out what you ask for, because you just might get it"? I am not quite dry yet, however, eager to begin our journey together.

*Part One*

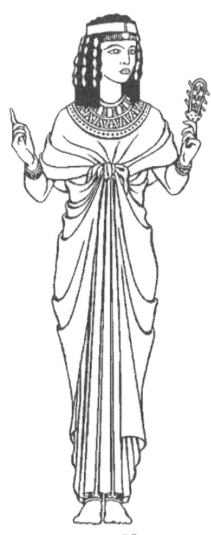

*The Lesser Mysteries*

# Desiring the Light
### (Story Line)

*At the core of my being exists a natural driving force that I could not ignore. The more I opened and listen to it the more it became me.*

*"Ask, and it shall be given you; seek, and ye shall find; knock, and it shall be opened unto you"* ~ *Matthew 7:7*

This time that we are all living in is truly auspicious. With the new millennium and the anticipated Golden Age drawing ever nearer, many more people are turning within, soul searching like never before, for what really matters, re-evaluating relationships with others, self and God. I would like to congratulate everyone who is reading this book at this time, for you are truly embarking on an awakening at a deep soul level regarding who and what you truly are.

Surely, the turn of the age has been one of the most talked about and anticipated events of late. Many visions of great change have been foretold, few promising much hope, most only portraying doom and gloom. It is certainly true that we need to change our approach as to how we live on this planet and with each other.

In our present time reference, this human body is the only vehicle for experiencing this time line that we have at our disposal for mass relationship pioneering in our present form. It is clearly prudent that we learn to navigate, shepherd and tend our Mother Earths vessel's delicate needs, as there are surely rough waters ahead. This actually begins with how we interact with one another; balance and harmony are extremely important ingredients in this stabilizing formula, as in any healthy biological system. The single most important factor for harvesting a plentiful yield is clearly *love*, an appreciation of life itself. The amount of caring and nurturing you spend on yourself will dynamically affect those around you. Therefore, the quality of life is in direct relation to the love and respect we show ourselves. It is pure and simple. Develop self- love, and the world will be directly affected.

Everything starts from within, as we shall see!

Before you can truly love anyone unconditionally, you must first love yourself completely. The intentions of this book are to assist you in discovering the most powerful force in the universe -- eternal true love. This is also the oldest quest under the sun, the pure desire to give and receive love unconditionally. It is at the core of every truth seeker. A big part of why you are reading this book is that you have knocked at your inner door, which is now beginning to open, revealing a beam of radiant light, which will warm your heart like never before. By the time you finish, that door will be wide open, and light will be a blanket of solace, wrapping you in the most fortified knowing of God's embrace. You will feel and know love of the purest kind; the love of the Creator and the most revered hidden wisdom will be yours.

My first maxim was "I am alive in the prophesied End Times," and it would be most beneficial to realize that you should be praised for being alive at this paramount time in history and for recognizing what your soul has guided you to. What you must understand is that you are preparing yourself for a major graduation. Many lifetimes have been spent in preparation for what is about to occur. It will come gradually at first, as each person begins to experience the truth of who they are. These pioneers will be referred to as "Teachers of Teachers." Soon there will be massive information outbreaks surrounding the divinity and truth of Self. It is hoped that eventually everyone will choose the highest path or road less traveled, and by traveling this path each person will discover their soul's mission.

That we should accept the "gift of salvation" on a soul level has been the desire of the Divine since the beginning of time, although the word "salvation" certainly is not the most appropriate, as we shall see, for we are truly not being saved from anything. More appropriate in this sense would be the theological word "atonement"; as AT-ONE-MENT.[2] The word that should actually be used to correctly denote this process in spiritual evolution is "realization", a total Self-Realization of the Self as Divine.

There will be a completely new understanding of what has perpetuated down through the ages as religion. For in the light of these new understandings, what religion promises as a reward after death for being "good" during this life will be seen as exactly the opposite: a trap to actually take you out of your power and away from the divine which is your birth right in this very moment. As you will see, everything that has been promised for a day of reckoning has always been available in the present.

Some of this information may be old for those of you who have already been carrying the torch for a quest of truth for sometime. What will be new is how we allow the experiences to transform us and activate our full blueprint, our "divinity". An opportunity now exists to not only become a part of the "new" paradigm shift, a shift in frequency to a higher level of consciousness and existence, a heaven on earth, but, more importantly, it is an opportunity to assist in this transformation and

---

[2] Middle English atonen, to be reconciled, from at one, in agreement. Excerpted from *The American Heritage® Dictionary of the English Language, Third Edition* © 1996 by Houghton Mifflin Company. Electronic version licensed from INSO Corporation; further reproduction and distribution in accordance with the Copyright Law of the United States. All rights reserved.

advancement of your own soul's evolution. The choice has always been whether or not you will choose your own highest road: *knock and the door shall be opened*, and *seek and you shall find*. The major difference now is that because of the culmination of the ages, cycles and alignments of stellar energies, this desired state will be much easier to achieve than ever before.

There will still be choices to make, even though you may be experiencing the most wonderful process of becoming. There will be those who believe the end has surely come, as they witness a total breakdown of all known systems. It is to this end that the Lightworkers serve, as examples and guides for others, becoming "Divine Perfect Human Beings", conscious of the multi-dimensional self and the innate, intimate connection to the source of all that is, the Creator.

This is more than just wishing to survive a pole shift or crustal displacement (i.e. ice age). It is the purest intention of really desiring to make a difference in the quality of existence. The differences are becoming more and more apparent to me, between choosing to make the shift and actually being a part of it. Much like the difference between doing something and just being it, or stating that there are things that first must be achieved before one can become all that they are, rather than choosing to just be in the state of knowing and therefore being the ISness of it. Thus stated, <u>there is definitely a difference between becoming an Ascended Being (simply one who resides in the next dimension) and becoming an Ascended Master in this dimension.</u>

It used to be my personal experience and belief that making the dimensional shift was something that I did not have to be concerned about. I always have had the understanding in my heart that if you were truly a good person, with an open heart and an open mind, you would come out just fine. This I have witnessed: everyone grows at their own pace. Opportunities are provided at the right time, for the right reasons and lessons. I believe the individual with an open heart will naturally resonate with the higher frequency, which continues to rise within our own 3rd dimension. The Earth's base resonate frequency is gradually preparing everyone for the shift. My personal desire has always been to be the best I can be and help others achieve the same goal. This desire and knowing has steadily increased over the years, as has my understanding of the quest that I am on. I have always held that I only wish to follow my highest path, but now I more fully understand where the road is taking me. I can honestly say that my path *is the way* of the "Ascended Master". I believe this is the soul's journey in its ascension and evolution into full Divine Realization.

What I wish to impart to you more than anything is some of the pearls that I have discovered and have been guided to find, as well as what has been purely gifted. A being that acquires the honored title of Master is one who has truly mastered this dimension and the vehicle or vessel used to inhabit it, the physical, emotional and mental bodies we most consciously know as self. The more we are able to understand the depths of this self the easier it becomes to connect with the true Self, the *Higher Self.*

Knowledge of self as Self is the perfection of creation that breathes a soothing relief of knowing that all is well, a feeling that warms your heart with an untold love for yourself and your intimate relationship with the Creator. Your own pure perfect self-love is the "truth" that will set you free. The veracity of this statement will become more and more clear and evident throughout this work.

# Story of 'In the Beginning'
### (Story Line)

*What I was guided to remember, already existed in the core of my being, within the fiber of my DNA, laid dormant a level of consciousness that existed since the beginning of time.* ✳

I have all but been obsessed with "In the Beginning" Stories. For over 22 years now, I always had my own inner knowing about the "Ancient of Days". I have also felt my deepest connections to the "Before Time" or the "Sept Tepi" also spelt "Zept Tepi", which in Egypt is the Beginning, "First Time" or "First Occurrence". I have had numerous experiences with past life recall and precognition, major triggers and revelations leading me to my true spiritual work. My entire life, to say the least, has been about finding and following my highest spiritual path, what can I do to serve, what can I do to grow more or become more. Many things have been revealed to me or occurred to me because of this strong desire. I am grateful to be able to draw on those experiences to help others. In constantly asking for my next step and the next personal issue to move through and release, I have been guided and prepared for this time, the revelations and my ministry.

For me, this is a time of truly becoming, of actually *being* who I am, most importantly completely and fully loving myself. There was a time when I was working through my rejection and abandonment issues and my sense of self-esteem definitely was low. Although I knew much about myself, I was not comfortable sharing, for fear of being rejected and/or invalidated. Even when I was feeling whole and good about myself, I very seldom would share my truest, deepest thoughts and feelings about my spiritual work and myself. So for most of my life I kept my inner understandings concealed deep within myself. Sometimes I could not believe what Spirit (the Creator) was trying to tell me. Then finally, when I least expected it, there it would be in plain view, proof of what I always knew.

It is ironic how we all know things but often do not believe even our own self-proof. Many years went by where I continued to watch for signs and then, after receiving them along with new insights, would still question myself. However, everything I have perceived as truth has proven out and come to pass, which is why I have come out and into my own, now fully empowered with self-love. I have finally healed all that was creating my self-doubt and fear, amazingly just in time. Rather perfect divine timing, wouldn't you say? It is truly just that, the most appropriate time for the message that I have to deliver. Until just recently it has literally been a process of becoming, right up until now, when it has become increasingly clear the best way to teach is by example and by sharing the direct experiences.

I would now like to introduce the individuals who, in this dimension, have been instrumental in preparing me for my mission by guiding me towards self-acceptance and greater self-confidence. I was only 19 when I had my experience of Self-Realization. And yet, I have found it interesting that this most wonderful great sense of Self was not enough to cause me to fully move into unconditional and complete self-love.

My dear friends have taught me several important things, but mostly they have confirmed what I already knew. Interestingly enough, considering that there must be reconciliation and balance between males and females for ascension, my two friends are of opposite gender. My greatest life lesson, without any question of doubt, has been that equipoise[3] is everything.

The first was an older woman, a master teacher, I will call Zoey. I was 27 when I met Zoey for the first time. She took one look at me and said, "I have been waiting for you. You are one of the 12 of the 24 conscious emanations." As she said this a chill went up my spine and down again. I had never heard that term before, yet I innately knew what it meant. I said, "Yes I know, I have always known!" The full extent and significance of what she told me will be elaborated on throughout this book. From that day forward, I really watched for Spirit to reveal the full story and understanding as I ever the more diligently searched for information confirming what I felt and knew to the core of my being.

When I was 33 I met the male version of Zoey whom I will call Cosmo. Amazingly, he was almost exactly the same kind of person or being as Zoey, and after 5 years of knowing this man, he revealed some very similar things to me regarding his awareness of my soul's heritage and past incarnations. Cosmo told me that he had knowledge of our meeting and of my mission before he even met me. The interesting thing about these individuals is that beyond what you might call "normal" psychic abilities, they both had what I refer to as "no subconscious barrier".

These two super psychics remembered everything they did while sleeping, if you can call it that. All their travels to other systems, dimensions and places, all the beings they encountered and everything that was said, always lucid and clear. If something significant was going on, anywhere they where tuned into it. I thought meeting someone like this was something that only happened once in a lifetime, but twice, I was beginning to get the picture even more strongly. Meeting Cosmo has really helped me with a few of my missing pieces, for I have been assembling this puzzle of

---

[3] e·qui·poise (ē'kwə-poiz', ĕk'wə-)

    1.   Equality in distribution, as of weight, relationship, or emotional forces; equilibrium.
    2.   A counterpoise; a counterbalance.

the Creation and Cosmography of existence, for well over ten years and his friendship and insight has contributed more than I can probably ever really convey to him.

What is astonishing to me is that I have always known I would write a book and yet, up until now I have never written any of this down before or told the story from beginning to end. When I began this project, I just let Spirit absolutely guide and inspire me. I was not actually sure when this story was to be told or how, but trusted that everything would work out when the time was right. Trusting has paid off, as everything is definitely absolutely perfect. The synchronistic events and flow of content received and remembered here are unparalleled in all my experiences and I am on fire with the truth of the message that is shared through the material.

So now then, let us begin to assemble this ancient wisdom temple. It is my greatest wish that it will unlock truth and full understanding for you as it has done for me. The intention is to fully acquaint you with the essence of the oldest recorded form of the mystery schools, as if you were actually going through the levels and degrees of initiation. The information and the knowledge will definitely have a profound effect on your body/mind system.

# Balance is the Key
## (Story Line)

*The entire message of this book is repeated in nature in a myriad of ways, reflecting the simple rules of the meta-mechanics of the universe, as it is within, so it is without – as it is above, so it is below.*

My whole life has been about the lesson of BALANCE; I have learned that one can never find true happiness, total fulfillment without this perfect balance, mentally, emotionally and spiritually healthy and whole on all levels. I am reminded of the words over the temple of Delphi, "Man know thyself," and it is not that commonly known that what is written directly beneath is, "Everything in moderation" in other words, in balance. This message is one that has resounded loud and clearly down through the ages, for those who wish to truly and completely find utter enlightenment and that ultimate sublime state of "I AM."

The single most essential equipoise, which must occur, is between the two inner aspects of the self, the masculine and the feminine, which represent the qualities of the essence of the universe. "Life force," the Divine electro-magnetic *Creation Essence*, is the result of the perfect, balanced blending of electricity and magnetism in a dance of ultimate equilibrium between the polarities of positive and negative. This represents the single most important key ingredient in the process of Ascension into Mastership or Self-Realization.

There is a unique distinction between the process of dimensional ascension and the actual process of ascending as a Master. The spiritual movement is now focused on the Dimensional Shifta transformation into a higher dimension, commonly called the fifth, where one becomes an ascended being, one who is consciously transferred from one reality to the next. The attainment of Ascended Mastership is another matter all together. It implies that one has become entirely causal in the third dimension, fully responsible for all of one's creations and not at their effect.

It becomes clear that the maxim "As above, so below," relates ultimately to the understanding that the love, acceptance and the integration of the two uniquely diametrically opposed counterparts is what diversely and divinely comprises the *whole*.

The deep desire to know God, and to experience the Creator's Love, is nothing more than the desire to totally love and accept the self. This is an almost unconscious, built-in response to life itself, the need to feel whole and complete, happy and fulfilled, a part of and not cut off from Source, unconditionally loved and not rejected. Essentially, the desire to be loved, that almost insatiable *need* to be loved, which we most often believe must be fulfilled by another, someone or something outside of ourselves, is nothing more than the Divinely inspired desire to love. Most seek this love of God from some great Supreme Being whom we conceive of as "up there," somewhere beyond the stars, rather than understanding that it is an intimate, innate, internal connection found just inside our own heart. It has been said that even God sought to know love, to be loved, that God *created*, in order to experience the feeling of being loved, and that therefore, our greatest spiritual accomplishment, our peak blissful experience is the returning back to God, the Source of all that is.

There is yet a deeper mystery, so self-evident and simple that it has hitherto remained hidden and little understood. It has been concealed purposely by those who stood to gain power or control by withholding it, and, on the opposite end, those who have known it have kept silent for fear of being ridiculed or rejected if they should divulge such a simple thing to be of such paramount importance.

However, this understanding does lie at the foundation of this great genesis experiment with duality. The embracing of the polarities, of the reciprocal aspects within and becoming one with all parts of self, in complete equipoise and perfect balance, is in fact *the way*! This is what truly sets us free and delivers us unto Eternal Life. It is the major first step and, as it turns out ironically, in a very profound way, it is the very last step as well.

The walk between the beginning and end is the journey of embracing an awareness of your divine birthright. The gift is finding the joy in each step along the way, as the Divine places each stone in synchronistic perfection upon your path to Divine Consciousness. Thus, returning to Source, as a reunited entity, both balanced and whole, is Completion, for ALL is ONE in the Mind and Heart of the CREATOR.

# The Grand Shift
### (Neo-History)

*My path and its potential has been clear within my heart for as long as I can remember, while time has never stood as a barrier constraining this recall, the great cycles of creations has marked its arrival.*

There are two very distinct occurrences taking place at this time in history. First of all, there is a great dimensional shift underway, an actual ascension of the planet. Those who choose to vibrate or resonate at the higher frequency, while yet remaining with the Earth, shall ride consciously into the next dimension or phase of universal evolution. Secondly, there is an opportunity to attain the honored title -- or perhaps better stated the sacred office of an "Ascended Master."

I would like to now focus particularly on the Dimensional Shift, an event that has been anticipated for quite some time. Many indigenous races have calendars, elaborate observatories and stone time keeping machines, which point to this time, the Aquarian Age, for some great change. This occurrence is unlike any previous pole shift, a phenomenon that is rather frequent in the overall scheme of cyclic planetary events, occurring every 25,827 years. The dimensional shift we are about to undergo is massive, an "Event Horizon" in comparison. (Reference Gregg Braden's book, *Awakening to Zero Point,* for greater detail and understanding about pole shifts and the history around this planetary activity.) In most cases, the calendars far outlived their creators' existence, which raises the question who and what were they for then, anyway? The calendars also all have one thing in common -- equinoxes. All the known oldest sites of civilization have megalithic monuments, which is accurately measure the exact time of equinoxes. They all keep detailed records of the occurrences of the equinox, counting the number from generation to generation. It is most interesting to note that the Great Pyramid has the number 25,827 exactly recorded in its dimensions, not once, not twice, but three times.

It is interesting to note that the equinoxes measured include dates preceding the origin date, or birthdates, of those civilizations. So what exactly were they counting, or more precisely, what were they waiting and watching for? We now know that they were interested in two things: the times of the pole shifts, and the time of the end of the great cosmic cycle. They were primarily concerned with the pole shifts, because these shifts often meant cataclysmic earth changes for which they attempted to prepare themselves. Moreover, they knew the number of pole-shift cycles required for the changing of ages, as well as the total number of cycles comprising the entire galactic cycle or greater ages. All of these cycles were broken down into 12 segments, the end of which marked one great galactic cycle or one year in galactic time.

They knew that each age brought great changes, both socially and geologically, and ultimately, that there would be a grand finale. This event has been prophesied by all races in one way or another. The Christians say: "It is the end of the world and judgment day." The Hopi say: "It is the beginning of the 4th world." The Mayans alluded to it as the beginning of galactic membership and the advancement of information. Each of these perspectives is an aspect of a multi-faceted truth. Most important is the understanding that there is a greater "Universal" cycle of measurement which corresponds with the culmination of the age and the galactic year.

What is being revealed here is that a "Grand Cycle" is now coming to an end. The completion will be referred to as the *beginning* of the 5th Universal Generation, or next Genesis Experiment. It is as though the great gears of the cosmological grandfather clock are lining up and the bell is striking midnight, with an angel coming out of the pearly gates, singing a divine song whose melody tells of tremendous change. What this signals, regardless of which ancient texts or prophecies you may be familiar with or examining, is a quintessential completion of a great divine cycle, *with a new heaven and earth*, literally a Divine Cosmic Event Horizon.

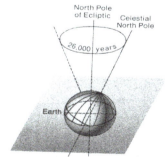

One-half rotation denotes the time for a pole shift, approximately every 12,000 years.

THE 7TH SEAL

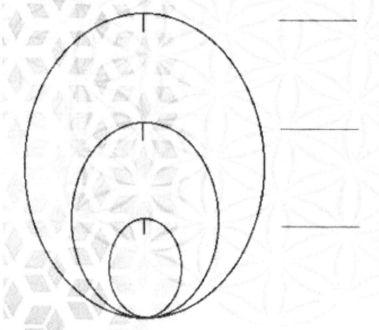

## Ascension is the Way
*(Story Line)*

*A proverbial golden feather of truth measures and weighs absolute certainty against relative perception. The only way to tip the scales of divine consciousness away from mere mortal servitude and sheer material influence is to experience a taste of the variety of divinity. This is accomplished by opening the mind to what is waiting to tickle your heart and soul just around every corner, if one would only pause long enough to feel the underlying truth inherent in one's own existence. The force of your Spirit, which is one with the all of creation, is within your every breath, stop and feel it and ask to have this Divine flow revealed in your life. Everyones world is constantly changing; growth can occur most naturally and effortlessly as the observer, this simply entails stepping back from the ups and downs of lives ever flowing sea of emotions, and breathing before thinking and acting. Your reality is ascending in this very moment, your first step up to meet the path before you is now only a choice away. When you completely desire to know your inner truth fully, you will become the balance between order and chaos in your life and the way to sovereign spiritual freedom and peace will be shown.*

Ascension, Enlightenment, and Self-Realization are all very nearly the same things. All indigenous cultures, as well as some religions, have their respective summit or peak achievement to be attained for spiritual purposes. They of course all culminate at the same place, for there are many paths back to Source. Some paths are highways and some are back roads; it is not the way you get there, but that you do which counts. Some ways are a little easier than others, and some ways are a little faster than others, but still it is very much the getting there that matters. Again, my greatest interest and the subject of my quest has been the approach that has been referred to as Ascension, or the process of oversoul transformation, the Ascended Master path, as previously referred to, meaning the ascension of the individual's consciousness back to the source of its higher collective soul group. One result of this is a greater connection with, and awareness of, the entire knowledge base as wisdom and experiences of the collective oversoul.

This is the way that I learned the most about past-life experiences in this lifetime, and it is the way that I personally recommend and teach. Ascension is the process of mastering this dimension, the $3^{rd}$ dimensional physical body as well as its inter-dimensional aspects, the mental body, the emotional body, the astral, and the etheric or spiritual body. These are five in number, and five is the number of the human being. This number has been revered in many ways by the mystery schools. We shall learn several fascinating things about this number and its relationship to *the way*, as we proceed.

It is most interesting to note that the Egyptians held the *way* as expressed in Maat, the "Goddess of Truth," in great reverence. The hieroglyphic sign of the Feather, against which the heart was weighed upon death in the process of judgment, was her symbol of truth. Within the concept of Maat, the scale of balances also exemplifies living in harmony with each other and the Earth. The act of judging the soul/heart concluded the life path with an examination of its content to determine whether or not the soul had achieved its desired level of evolution. This was defined as the summation of *the way* in accordance with time-honored ancient Egyptian practices, rites, and beliefs.

The overall ascension process (*the way*) increases the frequency of your body, raising it higher and higher. As this begins, you may become more and more sensitive to denser or lower vibrations, and you will find that you require adjustments in your life style to accommodate your new senses. This can involve many things from diet to personal activities, people you interact with, to where or what you do for a living.

Ascension in Mastery is the natural intended evolutionary process in which the soul as the Oversoul in Completion returns to the original state of a perfected human being. The word Hu-man is derived from a Sanskrit word and is translated as God-man. One of the main reasons so many souls want to be embodied now is to experience this state of becoming a God-person during this unprecedented dimensional shift, especially because the opportunity and ability to become an Ascended Master is much more accessible now due to the surrounding circumstances, as we shall see.

The process has begun for many people (light beings) and will actually completing for some very shortly. It is hoped that many will make this choice now. In truth, many are called and few choose themselves, as this is truly the ultimate free will choice, to choose the way or path back to your highest expression as a divinely conscious being of ineffable light and love. This is truly everyone's personal birthright. The consciousness shift will occur for many at this time, though the number of individuals who actually are prepared to shift with the required open heart could greatly be increased with every newly awakened "Master." All light beings (those spiritually aware or seeking same) will make the grade required for the frequency shift, or literally the dimensional shift, which ultimately the event horizon that will raise the consciousness or frequency of all forms, materially and etherically. The question remains how many will choose to really assist in the unfolding of this greater Divine Plan.

The Ascended Masters will help many after the shift as well, for as we become members of the Galactic Family, the Divine Plan really begins to unfold. The Race of Perfect Divine Human Beings will be the Ambassadors, so to speak, for the Kingdom of Light. This entails preparing and delivering the truth about what is actually taking place all across the universe at this time, as well as assisting in the harvesting or healing of the 'Great Banishment', the casting out, denial, avoiding, and branding of the Lucifer/Yaldabaoth beings as less than. Something similar to this also actually occurred between the males/gods and females/goddesses. We will be delving into these controversial subjects briefly.

The Divine sons and daughters of the Creators will guide the way for many races in other worlds, planes, and realms of existence into the higher levels of consciousness, on the journey home to Source. In the course of Earth's history there have been fewer than 2,200 beings that have ascended, many of whom have done this more than once on several different worlds. Ascension does not always occur in the incarnated state, although the criterion for Ascension has always been the same. The following best defines the requirements: discovery of who you truly are on all levels, integrating all aspects of your greater oversoul, mastering the 3$^{rd}$ dimensional form and coming to completely love who you are unconditionally, as well as seeing this aspect in everyone else as the unwavering selfless desire to show compassion, love and service to all the Creator's children. Finally, the most important key is to become a balanced male/female androgynous being. The latter is the main overall requirement, because this single accomplishment of unification lays within the Gnostic proverbial statement the *two become one*, which actually enables the full completion of the ascension process.

An understanding of this state of being and awareness prepares the oversoul for its transformation into its original Divine state. The oversoul may accomplish this in one lifetime or one thousand lifetimes, it is almost always different from case to case, but the requirements have always been that the soul must transition back into the original oversoul level or consciousness. However, now the window is wide open with the greatest celestial alignment supporting the assimilation of all energy into the omnipotent primordial ONE source.

Some of the most well known Ascensions or Ascended Masters have been Jesus, Buddha, St. Germain, El Morya, Kuthumi, Quan-Yin, Osiris and Enoch.

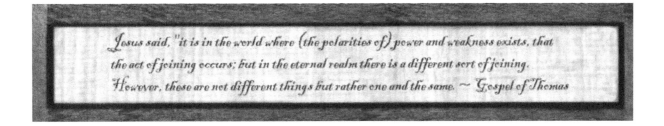

*Jesus said, "it is in the world where (the polarities of) power and weakness exists, that the act of joining occurs; but in the eternal realm there is a different sort of joining. However, these are not different things but rather one and the same. ~ Gospel of Thomas*

# Pistis Sophia
(Story Line)

*Wisdom, the most sought after virtue of the ages, has been kept hidden in the most open and perhaps obvious places, as well as behind what has been labeled less than or evil. The teaching of the ancient mystery schools reveals the lock and the key, the formula for the equation, the story of the keepers of wisdom and their resplendent ways of enlivening and enlightening the heart and soul. Herein lies the euphemism, knowledge is power, and those who attempt to attain either knowledge or wisdom (as power) without love will remain unrealized and dis-empowered. Any one virtue alone without the understanding that everything is energy and interconnected is derogatory to the evolution of the whole and will always be less than perfect. Herein are the keys to existing in harmony with the full spectrum of creation. Wisdom is often discovered in the misunderstood or misinterpreted parts of self. As we open the door unto our true selves we will be amazed at what has been most dishonored and disrespected, for it is the only thing that can set us free. The plain truth has always been mocked and played down for fear of the loss of control, this is not true power/wisdom, for real power is all knowing and all loving.*

It would be most beneficial to further emphasize the way this book will be presented. The chapter subtitles comprise the weave of the greater tapestry of the material (Story Line, Neo-History, Sacred Geometry, etc.), braiding a balanced presentation that will serenade a dance between the left and the right brain, which shifts from science to philosophy through artistically woven threads of logical, intellectually stimulating details, blended with my experiential story of self discovery, along with a visually artistic portrayal. Part One - **the Lesser Mysteries** - will lay the foundation required to support our Temple of Truth, which will be fully erected in Part Two, the Greater Mysteries, while the third section - the Greatest Story Never Told - is my own journey recalled through a divine reflection.

It may behoove you to allow portions of this material to simply speak to your soul on a subtle level. You might try to just sit with parts that silently call to you, receiving the intended transmissions of light and wisdom. Within these pages there are various activations that will be initiated through synthesizing the symmetry romance of the left and the right, the male and the female, the above and the below, and the inside and outside. The Egyptians held this universal reciprocal interplay so sacred within their tabernacle of truth that it was only to be orally transmitted. The Unity of ALL as ONE, with the Balance of the Divine Twins (King and Queen) as the central theme that outwardly displayed the harmony of the whole.

One of the main revelations that will be given in this work is the correlation and unique connection that Jesus had with the Egyptians. It is known that the Gnostics, who were the first followers of Christ, had a definite link with the Egyptians. The Coptics, for example, who were a branch of the Gnostics, lived in Egypt for several hundred years. Additionally, the fact that the Gnostic Scriptures were found in Egypt at Nag Hammadi in 1945 lends further support to the above postulation.

I will paraphrase one of the most auspicious passages from the Pistis Sophia (*Pistis Sophia means* **Faith Wisdom**, *literally faith through Wisdom, rather than blind faith in empty words.*) to preface the deliverance of a body of knowledge that was revered as the most complete and pure account of creation. This passage opens with the reference that it has been 11 years since Jesus *survived the cross.*

Directly before the Apostles a brilliant glowing sphere of light descends upon Jesus, having the appearance of wheels within wheels (*i.e.*, a spinning Merkaba, page 135). The Apostles, though startled, try to look at it to discern its nature, but are refrained by its resplendent magnitude and sheer opulence for it is more brilliant than the sun.

It had been five hours since Jesus had ascended in the light sphere when the reverse commenced. Jesus descended saying he had picked up his '*Garment of Light*', which he had put down to come into this world. This light vehicle (Merkaba), which was now at his complete command, was the means he used to travel to the Eternal Realm of the Light-Kingdom where He was shown all things. He said it was time to reveal *all things* to his disciples and that this was the first time "*all things*" would be fully revealed so openly. Jesus then said, *"This is because it is you 12 light-powers that will redeem the world in the end times." (Referring to the 12 creational level oversouls, as we shall see)* You will come to know and understand the full extent and nature of this most provocative statement within these pages.

Quoting the Gospel of Thomas (a Gnostic Scripture), with what Jesus must also have said at that auspicious moment, we now begin to unfold the ancient scroll to nourish and edify your beloved eternal soul.

> *"I will give you what eyes have not seen and what ears have not heard, what hands have not touched, and what has not come upon the human heart."* ♀

The material before you today represents the return of the long awaited *revealing of all things*, as Jesus taught it in his mystery school 2,000 years ago, as it was taught by many Masters through the annals and mists of time at the beginning of each astrological age (approximately 2,152 years or the greater zodiacal house of the precession of the equinoxes) down through history.

This material is actually released in its entirety just before every golden age (every 12,000 years) by the august sages and prophets of the time.

We will now continue with this type of information, my soul's remembrances, and experiences of how and what Sophia and Spirit guided me to unlock as the vision that God/Goddess placed within my heart. I have always had glimpses of this pure truth, as an innate knowing about many things within the nature of reality, although, it was not until I fully came to trust my personal experiences of Spirit and the Creatorship working directly in my life that the veils were completely removed from the grand vision eternally encoded in my soul. The core of this magnificent truth is that we all carry the vision or pieces of it and the Divine essence of Spirit within us, simply awaiting our pure trust, acceptance and surrender to blossom.

I can certainly attest to the validity of the following well-known quote.

*"Seek and you shall find, knock and the door shall be opened." - Matthew 7:7*

Could it be that there is new light to be shed on the age-old adage that "the Kingdom of Heaven is within you?" Perhaps this is one of the most profound utterances to ever fall from human lips, revealing the most basic truth that we are truly already DIVINE and ONE with the Mind and Heart of the Creator. All we really must do is actually realize this truth and feel the unequivocal Love in the here and now. This is Gnosis; the acquaintance with the Divine or knowledge of the essence of "All That Is" as Self.

This is most often easier said than done, as it has taken me several years since my First Realization to fully embrace and BE the divinity within me. This is one of the main reasons we have had mystery schools over the ages, not only to remind us of the truth, but also to heal and help remove the blocks and conditioning of the all pervading separation consciousness that has bound us to the illusion of duality and the polarity of good and evil.

# The Corner Stone in Phi
*(Sacred Geometry)*

*The key to it all is hidden within the ingredients and the way these seemingly lesser parts form the greater whole. This is seen in a myriad of ways throughout creation.*

At this time it becomes appropriate to take our first look at geometry. This will be our base foundation in this work; all of creation uses this natural mathematical universal language. It constitutes the fundamental building blocks of sacred geometry, the vibronics and frequency responses of all energetic wave fields that are the underpinning creational essence of all living existent forms of matter. This type of representation is apparent in literally every aspect of creation, from macrocosms to microcosms, from galaxies to molecules. The core golden thread that binds the fabric of reality together is the Fibonacci sequence. The sequence seen below is an array of numbers that is the algorithm or formula of life. It is the underlying key ingredient for what is referred to as the Golden Mean, Golden Section or Phi Ratio, which we will be going into in significant detail as we progress through this material. The Fibonacci sequence has its roots in ancient Hindu and Egyptian mysticism. It was reawakened into mainstream thought through a discovery by Leonardo Fibonacci of Pisa, Italy, a mathematician in the 13th century, who by counting the population and reproduction of rabbits discovered a number series from which one can derive the Golden Section or Golden Mean Rectangle and the Sacred Cut, which we now know was prevalent in all masonry construction of sacred temples throughout most civilizations.

The number sequence has some unique and profound characteristics inherent within it.

1 1 2 3 5 8 13 21 34 55

For example, the numbers are each the sum of the previous.

0+1=1  1+1=2  1+2=3  2+3=5  3+5=8  5+8=13  8+13=21  13+21=34

Things begin to get very interesting and amazing as the interconnectedness of all things begins to become apparent with the help of this number sequence.

As you contemplate the Phi Ratio, or Divine Ratio, you will begin to understand how there could be a universal nature language, a fabric that binds all creation together. This ratio is the quotient of the values derived by dividing each number in the Fibonacci sequence by the preceding number. This ratio stabilizes around 1.618034.

We can examine this phenomenon in a couple of ways to simplify the understanding.

The diagram of the graph below shows how a line is formed, which resembles a sine wave; we will later explore the power and cadence of this unique line or waveform. When this wave is placed on a computer and three-dimensionally animated, it may be spun, revealing many patterns, including the Golden Mean Spiral, which is shown below in its natural form as the Nautilus shell. Thus, this demonstrates the innate harmony or symmetry evidenced by this ratio.

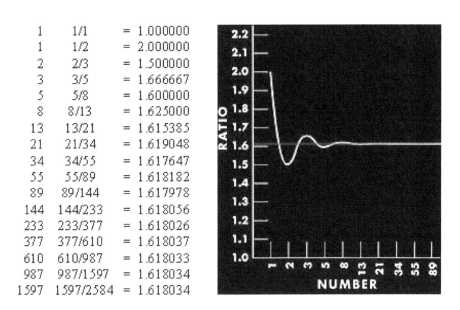

Above we see the stabilization of the phi ratio at 1.618 within the graph as a straight line proceeding infinitely out to the right from the quotient value of 55. With further study, as we shall see, an overall comprehension of the value of the numbers and relevant sequences begets an understanding of why Pythagoras espoused that numbers can define the entire universe, with each base number of 1 through 9 having a value, literally being comprised of colors, sounds, shapes, and their corresponding frequencies.

# Seeds of Life
### (Sacred Geometry)

*Mother Nature shares her secret formula for perfection. Here is the beginning of many signs that have always instilled delight, easing the mind into a thoughtless absorption of the beauty inherent in nature's oxymoron; the simplicity of complexity.*

With an understanding of the Fibonacci sequence and the characteristics of the Phi Ratio, we can clearly begin to recognize a pattern or method of symmetric Divine unfolding, evidencing a self-aware, self-generating matrix. When we look at nature, we can see the natural law of creation at work. Also, when we look at it through the lens of the sacred geometry of Phi, it becomes increasingly obvious that everything is in Divine perfection.

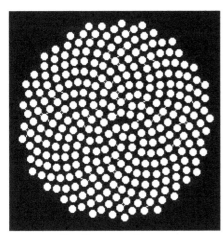 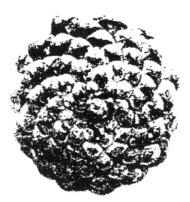 

Sunflower seed pattern (seeds detailed above)　　　Pine Cone Spirals　　　Nautilus shell

As you can see, nature best organizes itself into perfect symmetry using the Phi Ratio; referencing the Fibonacci as an algorithm, the universe best optimizes space and placement, producing harmony in creation.

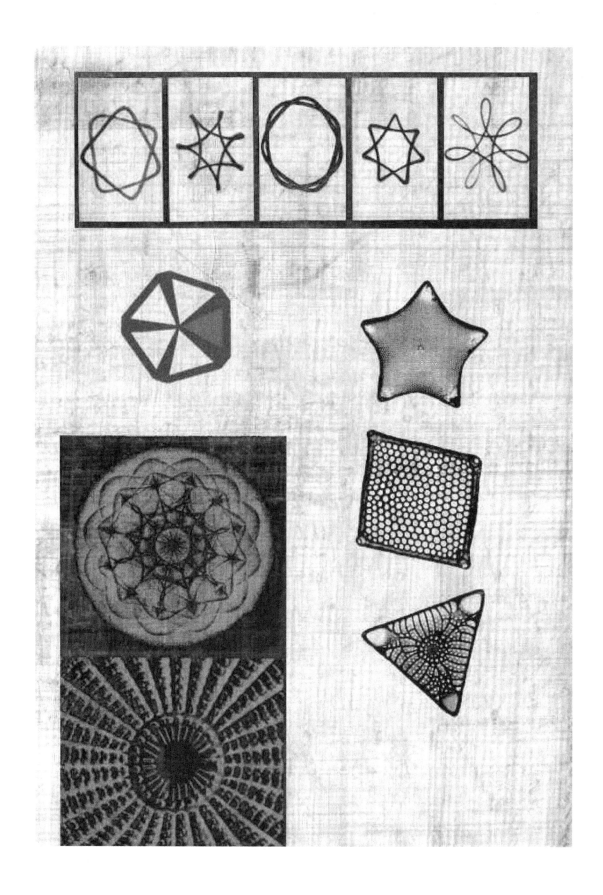

*The wisdom of the Egyptians reveals the keys to living in harmony with creation and all its unique parts. The golden age is upon us, as is the unveiling of the secret teachings of all ages.*

# Foundation of the Tree of Life
*(Sacred Geometry)*

*The keys and elements for deciphering the laws of nature exist in the patterns and signatures of nature. These codes and formulas literally exist all around us, continually reflecting our perfection. In order to attain the wisdom of the ancients we must open our minds and hearts and become aware of our entire existence. Only then can we truly master our kingdom.*

One of the most interesting things I have learned about the Fibonacci sequence is how bees like rabbits share the same genealogical tree, except for one very astonishing fact; the Queen bee does not require a male to make a female duplicate of herself. She literally has the ability to create via Immaculate Conception. I found this to be very interesting and showing a direct correlation to the origin and creation of the first beings of existence, as we shall see. This became the primary missing piece in my quest to assemble the greater creation puzzle. This is one of the foundational keys that bring all the pieces of this puzzle together to form a complete picture.

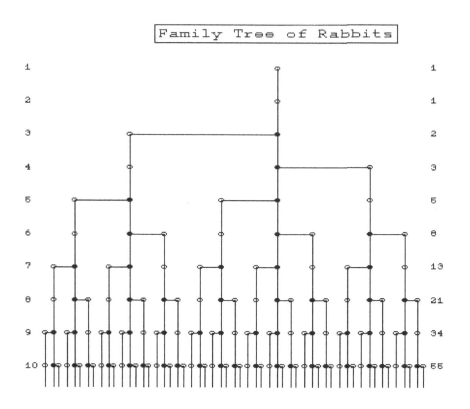

Some other very interesting information also adding to this picture or understanding, is that science has proven and performed a version of Immaculate Conception by pricking the egg of a female human being, whereby the metamorphic process of mitosis is induced, producing an identical twin or clone of the mother. Below is a glimpse of the basis for the actual Fibonacci Tree of Life. This is the first version and vision that I saw when contemplating the relationship to creation itself. It represents the four gates or directions, as well as the four prime elements of air, water, fire, and earth. There is also a visual resemblance to some of the Hopi's artwork, which tribe is also highly attuned to nature and Spirit.

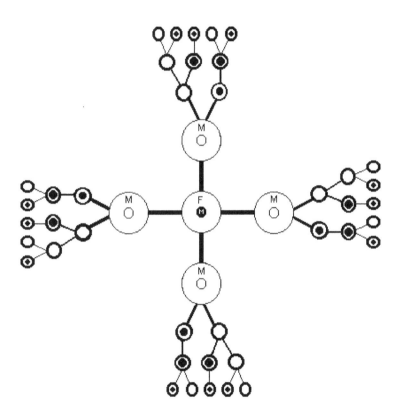

This depiction follows the natural flow of creations unfolding commencing in a series of movements that starts with the four cardinal directions. We will come to understand a great deal about these archetypal energies that are at the core of creation, representing the primordial pillars of divine stability and balanced harmony.

# Cosmology of the Creator

### (Neo-History)

*Were Jesus and his followers really called Christians? A detailed study of history reveals many things that are in contradiction to what is commonly believed today. There once existed a very devout group of wisdom seekers that lived in and around the land of Egypt and Palestine during the last and first centuries of a time when the calendar was being redefined by the Romans: 0 A.D., which represented the time "After the Death" of Jesus Christ, was the most pivotal time in all of recorded history when beliefs and realities where been formed by the force of a sword. The wisdom and truth seekers continued to desire to follow age old ways, while the power and knowledge (based on intellectual pursuit and material satisfaction alone) seekers sought to root out all obstacles in the way of the advancement of organized civilization. The true followers of Jesus survived 300 years of persecution before they where finally eradicated from the Roman Empire. These blessed souls where know as the Gnostics.*

The Creation Story that best fits or follows how everything actually unfolded from the Absolute Perfect Self-Existent Being is portrayed in the earliest of the Gnostic Scriptures. This is from the spiritual sect simply known by the Gnostics. This term was Greek for knowledge (as gnosis) and by the Gnostics themselves as a knowingness of a conscious connection to the source of all that is. The definition of gnosis will be expanded upon, as we discover a deeper meaning that has been kept hidden. The group known as Gnostics was the true first followers of Christ Jesus. They revered the Secret Doctrine of the Egyptians. Many of the scriptures were actually written by the Apostles themselves incorporating the wisdom that they learned about the Egyptians from the Mystery Schools still in existence than and Jesus himself. These secret teachings, unlike the New Testament, which were compiled at least 100 years after Jesus lived, were written closer to the time of Christ (approximately 50 BC) as simple sayings rather than parables.

These Gnostic Scriptures ended up being buried in clay jars in the sand of Egypt around 300 AD. This was prompted because the Romans (Constantine, the Emperor who converted the Romans to a version of Christianity.) and the early

Church fathers where killing off the Gnostics as one of their greatest threats or adversaries. This act of preservation was necessary, because much of the core material around the Gnostic faith was diversely different from what the Church wanted people to believe.

These scriptures, encapsulated in the forgotten layers of time and sand dunes, have lain undisturbed or tampered with for approximately 1,700 years. Some of the writings suffered damage obscuring portions of their deeper truth, though the majority is crystal clear in the deliverance of a very profound message of who we truly are. There ended up being several variations of the Gnostic beliefs, each with a slightly different interpretation on the major themes, for example; creation myths, how to be redeemed, and the mission of the Savior. Mostly they all follow the basic premise that we are divine spiritual beings trying to return home. Revealing the existence of great teachers, consciously connected to the whole truth, which were sent down to earth to remind us of our heritage and help us ascend back to that primordial Divine exalted state.

The New Testament states in several different places that Jesus taught the multitudes in parables and the disciples in open truth, although, some meanings were still shrouded in deep mystery as we will come to see. It has also been reported there were two versions of the gospels, one for the multitudes and one for the Elect. I very strongly believe that the Gnostic Scriptures are the secret Gospels which reveal the truth openly for those who have ears to hear. It appears through great research that the truth was only recorded, as they understood it. This is definitely the case with much of the New Testament. In addition to the actual writers, transcribers, or translators who had their own understanding acting as a filter, which in some cases caused them to slant, taint, distort, or even completely change some of the original meanings or teachings -- not to mention some very deliberate manipulations that we will look at briefly.

This can also be related to what can happen to information received through the process of channeling, which was exactly what prophets were in those days. Just as there are some very clear prophets today, they are prophets who have surrendered to God's will. Those channelers or prophets that are not clear in their transmissions have not surrendered to the will of God or have not dealt with their personal issues. In simple terms, the information comes to them filtered by their emotional body. There were similar cases back then, for there truly is nothing new under the sun. We will be looking at some of the most obvious areas where a deviation from the most likely unfolding of creation, based on the laws of universal metaphysics, seem to differ greatly from the most probable occurrences in relation to the geometry of nature. I also wish to point out this is not actually theoretical work, but guided by my connection to Source and Spirit, though largely based and reinforced by all the evidence demonstrated here. It will behoove you to receive a bit of a background on the Gnostic Creation story, in order to set the stage, so to speak, within the natural law framework.

Obviously, it all starts with an Absolute, Omnipresent Perfect Divine Being or Spirit Presence, which literally just IS. This being essentially realizing its self-awareness and self-conscious state recognizes that it is in perfect harmony and unity within its self. Therefore, with this understanding it chooses to experience separation or polarity consciousness. This desire creates a being outside of itself, which is referred to as the first principle. As the story goes, this being is a Parent entity, which creates a twin son and daughter. These children are referred to by many names; the Divine Twinship, the Perfect Human Being, the First Begotten, and the Eternals. Then as the story goes these beings created a race of children; the children of the light - *the Perfect Race*. These children are what the bible refers to as the 'sons of man' - *the immovable imperishable race*. There are several other references to names describing beings and states of being. Which at first do not appear to really fit into any special or particular place, for example the 24 invisible ones, the self-begotten ones, the three-tripled powers, and the unpaired ones.

When you look at the information within the framework set up by the Fibonacci sequence and the understanding that is put forth here of the Eternal Race and Realms of Light, this is where things start to make sense and almost naturally fall into place. These texts also offer a viable explanation for the creation of the being commonly known as "Lucifer" who is referred to in the Gnostic belief system as "Yaldabaoth." This is one of the most significant parts of the overall creation story and it is quite possibly the most important aspect in the entire scheme of things. As we investigate the role of this being, we shall see that all experiences ultimately involve the aspect that this being represents and embodies.

First, we will need to look at the foundational structure, for the most part; this is well depicted with the descriptions given in the Gnostic Scriptures.

# The Fruit of Life
*(Neo-History)*

*In order to build a temple of truth there must a solid foundation that the fundamental tenants of a structured belief or reality can stand upon. Nearly all the ancients agreed upon a semblance of commonalities when it came to the beginning of creation and its creatures, predominately the humans. This either suggests that they all came from one older source or that they reached this understanding through their spiritual faculties. For example, Shamans, one of the oldest known priests and healers, glimpsed the seeds of creation in altered states, both naturally induced and by an intense innerward focus. A key to fully discovering SELF lies in the acceptance of some point of origin that demonstrates an intention or pattern that can be followed, traced and understood, or perhaps in some way felt, seen or experienced, verses mere intellectual acceptance.*

"*In the Beginning*"...These words are very common, and we actually find many similarities to the main ingredients in the creation myths of all cultures. The Egyptian Book of the Dead, for example, which is a very ancient body of work (circa 4000 AD or older), which had been copied down generation after generation states; "*I am the Eternal, I am Ra, I am which created the Word, I am the Word.*" You will notice that this very much resembles the Bibles first words. "*In the Beginning was the Word, and the word was with God, and the Word was God.*" These are very true statements about the beginning acts of creating. The Word, which is translated from Logos (Logi), has the meaning of taking action, the early translation, as well as the French give the meaning as, "The Verb." This is the ACTION of the interaction of Intellect and Spirit, through intention in a balanced act of manifesting as Creation.

Simply any manifestation can be accomplished through focused thought and pure intent. The *intent* is what imbues the thought with Spirit, thus manifesting it. So then, these are very direct creational phrases, which deliver the meaning of a Creator creating a creation, which is an expression of the Creator and an experience for the Creator as self in Self. As the essence of Spirit and Consciousness permeates the Self's creation, or more simply the Creator, in its Creation. The Father or Parent entity, having the foreknowledge of its self as Self, being begotten for the experience of separation and polarity consciousness continued the process of replicating a copy of itself. Therefore, the literal fruit, which hangs from the tree of life, are its creations; these are the Children or actually Co-Creator beings. These beings actually did all the rest of the creating; the races, the galaxies, the solar systems, the planets, etc. These Divine Children are finite in number. The original "*Eternals*" are the first two tiers or branches of this tree, the parent entity and its twin children. This layer of creation and its beings are referred to as the first cause. This is also referred to as the Twin Rays, literally the twelve archetypal frequencies of the fabric of creation.

(Reference the picture on the next page as to better understand this phase of creation.)

During this emanation, the first truly begotten being was the highest aspect of Jesus' oversoul; Sananda Kumara, as the first Divine Twinship, This being was created both male and female; as perfect reflections of self in Self. (The Father figure was more of a reflection of source; therefore, the Gnostic's name; unbegotten.) This Divine family was referred to as the Triple Powered One; Mother/Father, Son and Daughter (with son and daughter as one and the same). Unlike further emanations at this time there was more conscious awareness of self within self in the beginning, as male and female perceptions developed and a more profound separation or split into polarity existence happened. This is where the inherent feeling of being separated or cut off from source truly comes from, for the full awareness of the self in Self became much less. This is what the fall from Grace was really all about. Leading to what would eventually become the perception of being seemingly lost as the fractualization or fragmentation of the essence of self-continued to split down through the Tree of Eternal Life. Nevertheless, the connection to source and Spirit of the inner self remained, and remains to this very day, right down to this very gross/dense material plane.

The nature of this great split caused or created the diverse polarities, a separation from the above and the below, resulting in an apparent disconnection from Spirit into Matter as two opposite energies; one male and the other female - the Genesis Experiment.

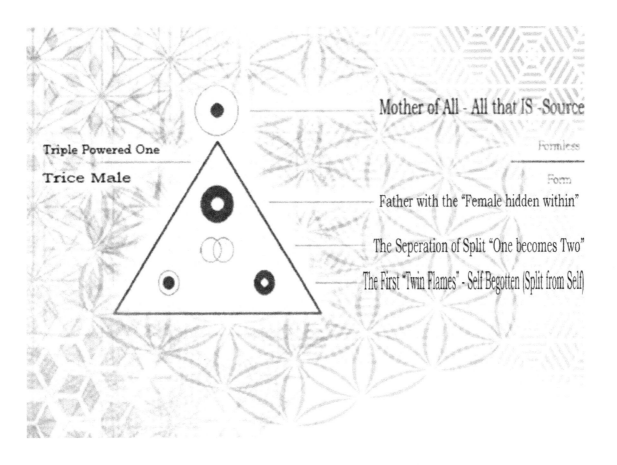

# Was he a she?
### (Neo-History)

*Everything in the universe is a reflection or sub-category of something else, a literal holographic part of the greater whole, where a copy of everything, at least in the pattern and frequency signature, exists in its totality. Hence the phrase "as Above so Below", which reveals the macrocosm and microcosm reflective nature of all existence. While this is one very significant key to understanding the formula inherent in creation it is incomplete without the knowledge of the laws of reciprocity. This is in essence the result of cause and effect, or karma, in effect, what goes around comes around. Another extremely relevant aspect to this fundamental tenant is that everything has an exact opposite, a counter balancing component that holds all of our perception of existence in place. So, for every action there is a reaction, this is essentially the law of order in the universe, supporting that everything has its equal reflection or expression, which maintains the spectrum of duality from white to black across all levels of energetic gradation, both in perception and measure alike.*

With a basic understanding of the Fibonacci sequence, let us begin to apply it to the creation story and see how it literally becomes the Tree of Eternal Life. The process of discovery while doing this work has been extremely profound not only within me, but also in terms of attuning to Spirit and following guidance, and the queues of synchronicity. I have never felt so supported and connected to a story that seemed to be unfolding right before my very eyes. This creation story as it has been revealed to me starts with a woman or mother, a female aspect predominately as the Absolute Most High Creator; The Great Divine Virgin.

The Gnostic Scriptures and the Egyptians have for the most part preserved the closest representation to what I have known and been shown by Spirit to be the truth, in terms of what can best be understood. Recognize this is best described as story or a frame of reference to define the energies of Creation, which from a linear standpoint is rather cumbersome to say the least. For the most part as humans, we require a linear portrayal, a story containing all the characters and plot to more fully comprehend the divine plan, which is far greater than just this dimension and is frankly more multi-faceted than our human minds perception can fully perceive, in its present form or state. Therefore, with that understanding put forth lets continue the story.

In the Beginning, the Self-Existing Divine Being, the Mother of All, had her "Great Emission" or birthing of a mirror image of herself. This is referred to as the "First Great Mystery" by the Gnostics. Many postulations exist about what the reason for this expression outside of self was really all about.

The most widely accepted is concerning the desire to experience love. Although, it is not too much of a leap to suspect there is a deeper or more complete, larger picture that everything is connected to, including her. We shall look more closely at this story/theory from several perspectives and its substantiating foundation later on in this work.

Moreover, the reflection of herself, which was a reversed mirror image, actually became a sentient being, which was Male in nature, although, having the image or rather energy of the Female creator within it. The Divine Mother Principle also actually had the Male within herself as well, hence the mirror image of the reversed Male polarity with a masculine awareness at the forefront of his consciousness, yet containing Spirit (or the feminine principle) within.

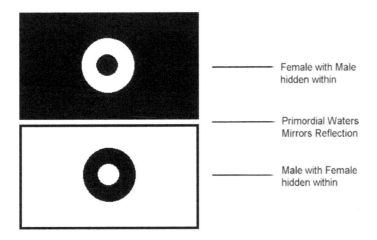

This primordial birthing process has the Mother Creatrix replicating a copy of herself, but turned inside out, so to speak, as a negative image. The creation was not linear, for it took place in a space that was without time or reference to direction, for nothing else in this void was pre-existent. The description of this creation, of a first principle, appears from the scripture, as a top down type formation. Later references in subsequent Gnostic Scriptures confuse and negate this type of single, one after another outpouring. This is where the understanding of the Tree of Eternal Life and plain guidance by spirit reveals that she made this great emission in 3 movements; the first was an emanation in the four directions. These are the four cardinal directions, the four prime elements, and the four gates referred to in many scriptures, including the Gnostic creation myths. She repeated this process 2 more times by turning from within her own reference point. Here it would be helpful to envision a three-dimensional sphere, with symmetric nodes or nodules geometrically placed and unfolding. Thus creating 12 beings that are the father figures or what is referred to in Gnostic Scriptures as the parent entity, for it also was both male and female. This is where the text refers to this being as an *androgynous male*, but again consciously aware of self as a Male.

This is very interesting since androgynous means both male and female. This may be their way of expressing the male energy as being on the forefront. Several Gnostic sects did not openly attribute the self-existent being as female. (We will see that this truth became suppressed, as it was the sacred sublime core wisdom of the Mystery Schools, hidden deeper and deeper as time went on, even in the first 50 years AD before the persecution of the Christians and Gnostics.) As I did this work, the clues and synchronicity of the feminine origin continued to present itself and supported the hypothesis I held within, which was later greatly supported and reinforced by the Egyptian material that was revealed by my own soul's recognition of truth. Mainly, the portent of a Female aspect or Goddess principle has many secrets or mysteries to reveal in the overall scheme of things. This truth continued to be proven and self evident, as I began to piece the puzzle together guided by Spirit's all-knowing invisible hand, as my inner knowing of being an advocate for the "Return of the Goddess" was undeniably proven.

One thing which caught my attention the most was that the numbers of all the sacred ingredients of an esoteric nature and the significant features of the creation stories could be found in the way the Fibonacci Tree of Eternal Life grew or unfolded. As I fully moved into the flow of what was being presented, completely embraced its truth, I was truly amazed at the relation and depth of the connections and the clarity it brought to the entire material that had been rolling around in my head for some time. Now let us take an actual look at the cosmography of creation, and an actual break down of the levels and the beings that reside in them.

As we continue to swing the door open to the ancient mystery school, we will discover the full meaning of the following Gnostic Scripture saying.

Images are visible to human beings, and the LIGHT within these is hidden by the Fathers Light. It will be disclosed, that his Image is hidden by his LIGHT

*Overview of invisible realm*

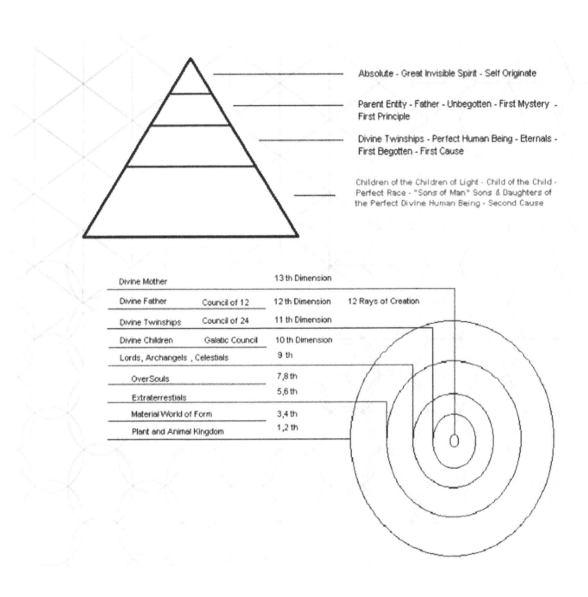

This is a visual depiction of all the current information combined with the creation model.

Mary said, "My savior, describe the Twenty-four invisibles. What is there type and quality of their light?" Jesus answered her, "There is nothing in this world that I can compare them to. I know of nothing that I can liken them to. I will simply say that one of the invisibles would be nine times greater than heaven and the sphere above it, including the twelve Aeons, just as I indicated to you once before. In this world there is nothing brighter than the light of this Sun, yet, the Twenty-four invisibles shine ten thousand times greater than the light of this Sun, as I have told you before. Truly the light of this Sun pierces many veils and regions, but the light of the glory in the region of the Virgin of Light shines ten thousand times greater than even the Twenty-four invisibles and the great Forefather. Therefore Mary there is nothing with which to compare the Twenty-four invisibles." ₮ Pistis Sophia

# 144 Children of Light
### (Neo-History)

*When a close examination of the elements and there respective labels are correlated against a foundational understanding of the primary essence of the whole a very interesting observation can be seen. The underlying geometry and number configurations that are inherent in the depiction of creation are replete with the markings or makings of a grand design evidencing the presence of vast intelligence.*

We find much of the esoteric mythology or etymology of creation echoing this sort of bifurcation from a single source. The primeval family birthed the Divine Twinships, continuing to emanate from the Parent entity until there were 12 sets, with each pair splitting into its respective polarity. This occurred until there were a total of 12 males and 12 females, known by the acolyte *"24 emanations of the Great Invisible One"* of the *"24 invisible ones."* This is what I innately knew of as the *"12 of the 24".* These are the *"Eternals"* who created everything else. This is the "Treasury of Light" where Jesus and his Twin are the first begotten, not the only begotten, as the Bible would have us believe. Within the last house, at the end or last quadrant of this Divine Zodiac is the <u>24th Mystery</u>; Sophia and her Twin -Sanat Kumara. This is where the phrase, *"the First will be last and the last will be First"* begins to play out, as we shall come to see this maybe one of the greatest mysteries and metaphoric utterances of all times.

The *'Children of Light'* are the offspring of this invisible eternal realm; they also created the luminaries or *'Oversouls'* to inhabit the material densities, as well as other dimensional realms. So this means the children are the projections of source consciousness, as souls, that are experiencing the creation; thus the name: "Children of the Children of Light."

These are also representative of the angels, the perfect human beings who soar to the highest realms, hence the wings on beautiful people, and it has been said that they are not male or female. It is interesting to note that the number of creator and co-creator beings is 72; there are 36 males and 36 females in the first 3 levels of the Tree of Eternal Life. (Reference the figures below) The number 72 is very sacred and can be found in many places, such as; the 72 names of God, 72 degrees of the precession of the equinoxes, the number of orders in the Melchizedek mystery schools, the secret keys of Enoch, the 72 degrees descending and ascending on Jacob's latter, 72 nations of God, 72 conspirators of Seth (who was Osiris' slayer), and the 72 extended disciples of Jesus.

Moreover, the halving of 144 produces an equation of 72 + 72 = 144. It is also very interesting to note that the number 144 is the number of the beings on the 12th level of the tree of life. Additionally, note 12 x 12 = 144. The number 144,000 can also be found in this tree as the 144 original oversouls, which are the projected emanations or souls for experiencing the creation their parents created. The emanations are seen as 1000 souls per each oversoul, resulting in the number 144,000.

*(Note: As we become ever the more familiar with numerology, you may desire to reread portions of this book for a deeper understanding of the interconnectedness of all things. For example, notice that almost all the numbers here ultimately add up to 9; for example: 7 + 2 = 9. This will become even more meaningful, as we begin to fully understand why nine is the number of completion. For example, how many months are in a pregnancy?)*

# Creation of Life
*(Sacred Geometry)*

*Further investigation of the central theme behind the creational force that cast this model of existence reveals additional interconnections between numbers, shapes and concepts.*

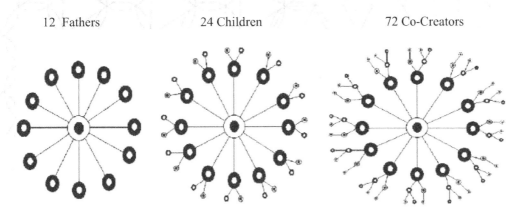

12 Fathers        24 Children        72 Co-Creators

The number 72 is most sacred and there are very sensible reasons as to why. The sacred science of the Egyptians knew that this number was an intrinsic part of the formula or ingredients of creation. When you take a circle (360 degrees) and divide it into 10-degree sections, for 36 divisions or decans, this is the Neteru or deities of the Egyptian Zodiac. This can be further viewed as 72 by the applying the polarity of genders to the decans. You then would have a male and female energy within each decan, which results in a splitting of the decans house or section into two sets of 5 degrees. Now you would have 36 male aspects and 36 female aspects; 36 + 36 = 72. We will see this same type of pattern or logic throughout much of the sacred geometry in the appendix; the meta-mechanics of Genesis.

In the diagram below notice the number of males to females in the unfolding of life. It would appear that the extra Females (they are represented with black centers) are the mysterious *"unpaired ones"*. It would also seem as though there is some sort of inherent contingency plan built into the overall latticework, which could be referred to as the Goddess's redemption plan or the Return of the Goddess. We will delve into the meaning of these topics in later chapters.

It would appear that this has something to do with when an Avatar is born into the world to remind the masses of who we are. This type of birthing is an Immaculate Conception from the unpaired Goddess personification. It produced a more conscious connection to the oversoul, resulting in a direct remembering or untainted knowing of absolute truth. There are 133 unpaired ones in each of the branches, which continue down to the 144th level, this is a seven numerologically, which continues to bring it all back to Spirituality (the numerological value or meaning of 7). We will see this theme repeatedly. Again the unfolding follows the 1,2,3,5,8,13,21,34,55,89,144 sequence, notice that this is 11 levels by the way, another extremely significant number esoterically. This number is derived by not counting the first one, which would be source, rather than a level, while including it reveals the number 12, the number of divine dual Creators.

THE 7TH SEAL                    54

# Creational Flow - *The Divine Unfolding*

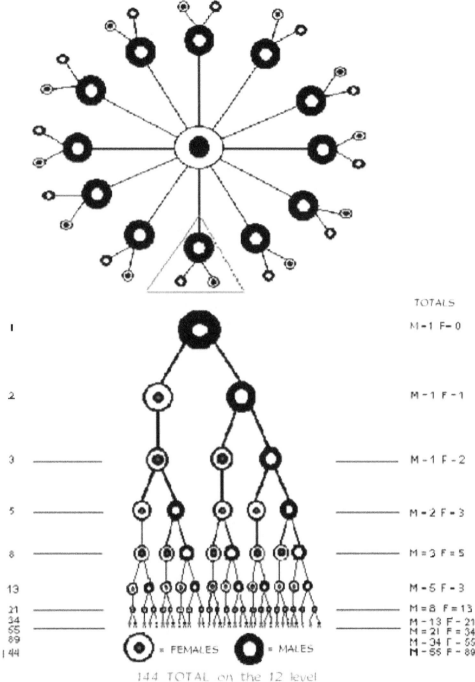

144 TOTAL on the 12 level

*Jesus said, "The heavenly human has many offspring, more than the earthly. If the offspring of Adam are many and yet die, how much more numerous are the offspring of the perfect human beings, who do not die but are being born every minute?"* ~ Gospel of Phillip

THE 7TH SEAL

# Let there be Yaldabaoth
## (Neo-History)

*How many ways can one spell the essence and meaning of GOD? Are there enough letters in the alphabet to adequately express the divine intelligence behind all of creation? Is it possible that such a superior or supreme being could exist that is solely responsible for every iota of seemingly precise order evidence in nature and creation itself? Does absolute divine intelligence represent just one end of the spectrum, and without an awareness of the whole, is literally ignorant of its overall place in existence?*

In the Gnostic creation myths we find Sophia creating a being called Yaldabaoth, although when you really look at all the remarks about the female it becomes apparent that there are some very blatant flaws in congruence regarding the nature of what becomes the obvious truth about Spirit and the geometrical natural expression of Mother Nature. Perhaps these were misinterpreted or misunderstood in relationship to the true nature of "*SPIRIT*" or perhaps the very strong influence of the patriarchal masculine dominance present at the time overruled the truth. This would cause an intentional cloaking of the truth about the Goddess by the mystery school to conceal the deepest wisdom for those who could fully understand and decode the pure truth through their Gnosis. It is due to this that the story remains curiously contradictory. It will become ever the more clear that various spins and reversals have been applied to sacred teachings throughout time for control purposes.

In the beginning when the first begotten ones of the invisible eternal realm, the Creator Beings, began to create beings after themselves, something unexpected happened. Or was it?

As the story goes, Sophia created a child without her mates consent. This child was defective or imperfect; the Gnostics called this event the "defect" in the Female or that the Female was in "error". Very interesting considering that she is also referenced as the "*Perfect One*" in other areas of the same scripture.

(It is most interesting to note that the words; perfect, spirit and goddess all add up to 73 or 10/1)

When you analyze the way the divine geometry unfolds, it is apparent that the natural perfect order or the "Wisdom" of Spirit follows a very precise unfolding. It would seem that this inherent pattern is not a defect or error at all but the pure intention of the ineffable Creatrix; the Mother principle herself.

It may be true that the patriarchs infiltrated these teachings as well to suppress the importance of the female goddess aspect at its source, so to speak. For if you view the story of the creation of the Lucifer being, through this new geometric lens of understanding things become much clearer.

The story would go more like this. The Female aspect of the last pair of the 24 Divine Twinships, Sophia or Wisdom, created a daughter after the same way she had known that she and her brother had been created, which was a natural act and way for her to procreate as well. She did this without any effort or interaction with anyone else; i.e. "Immaculate Conception". When her brother/mate had seen this, he believed he should also be able to create a being in this same manner. When the male aspect of the divine Twinships attempted to beget a being/child for himself, and in his own image, something was created that was not expected.
Considering that Sophia was considered to be perfect, along with other references stating that what needed repair was the completion of the male, as we shall see. It would appear that what is more likely to have happened is as follows.

From this male progenitor a being was created that was very unusual in appearance, for it did not resemble them, it was a male but it appeared to be blind because it could not see them, or was unable to perceive them. This male was also devoid of an inner female aspect. It had a soul but was imperfect because it lacked a Spirit, and in this manner, it was deformed. (The 'defect' in the female that the Scriptures mention may actually be referring to the missing Spirit aspect of what had been created.) It also existed outside of the invisible realm, for it was not aware that anything else existed, it was alone. It was definitely male, and very intelligent, all mind and no heart. So much so, that he was out of balance for he completely lacked any emotions or feelings what so ever. It was said that he had the body of a snake or reptile and the face of a lion. He was the first creation that was visible, not of or in the invisible realm, thus the inability to see its parent.

He was called Sakla and Yaldabaoth, for Sakla or Samual[4], means, "blind one" and Yaldabaoth means, *"Authority over the Armies of Power"* i.e. Rulers. There is one additional meaning that strongly suggests the nature of this being; the youth that goes forth here and there. This being had many talents and powers; he was also very capable of *creating*. He began to experiment with the manifestations of his mind, as he worked with the natural laws of geometry he become quite gifted at fabricating form and cosmic matter. After some time he longed for someone to show off his great creations to. He was also lonely for he sensed that *something* was missing. He was not sure what, but felt certain that a part of him was somehow lost, incomplete or unknown. (Does this sound like a familiar theme?)

His great desire and deep longing through the determination to experience something other than himself and his creations enabled him to create a son. This male, named Sabaoth, was created identical to him, intelligent and soulful, but lacking emotions/spirit. This creation brought him great satisfaction. They explored his creations together and eventually fashioned many more in hierarchical cooperation. They were content for sometime. Meanwhile the invisible divine Twinships continue to create, as well, although with the learned wisdom of the interaction with their counterparts. They created a myriad of perfect human beings, the 'immovable, imperishable race of the invisible eternal realms."

The Spiritless father and son team also created galaxies, solar systems, and planets themselves. Several cycles of cosmic time had passed, when Yaldabaoth's longing for something more returned. He desired a mate, a companion, he was lacking in love and sought to know what he missed or innately knew was missing. This would become a trait that was genetically passed down through his creations and soul fragmentation. In this way, it was a part of the conscience matrix of the whole. This being and all its creations would become the polarity or adversary, which would add balance to existence. It would provide a choice of freewill in experiences and expression setting up the full spectrum of duality.

This being and its races would create many things to try to satisfy and satiate its MIND, all of which were manifestations outside of itself. This way of externally seeking is what is commonly referred to as 'the way of the Lucifer Rebellion.' This is a way of rebelling against the truth, that there is a power greater than itself or that it is actually part of the collective whole. Overcoming this aspect of ego is the

---

[4] There is a strong resemblance here to the sons of Heaven from the Book of Enoch. The chief ruler of the angels that descended on the mountain of Armon (Hermon) was called Samyaza.

single greatest key to unlocking and removing the genetic programming that has kept us as humans from being completely conscious and empowered by the holistic harmony and balance of our connection to the ONE SOURCE. As an intricate part of the whole, for the Perfect Divine Human Race is our natural eternal birthright.

 *"Light and Darkness, life and death, right and left, are siblings; it is impossible for them to be separate. Accordingly, the good are not good, bad not bad, and life is not life, nor death death. So each will be dispersed to its original source. However, things that are superior to these are indissoluble, for they are ETERNAL!"* ~ *Gnostic Gospel of Phillip*

*Creation of Yaldabaoth*

# Eve gives life to Adam
(Neo-History)

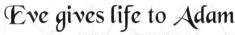

*Are the Romans in actuality alive and well today, continuing to suppress the greater truths, effecting the prevention of the resurgence of a spiritually aware and solely (souly) aligned civilization? If central truths where turned inside out and reflected to us backwards would one still be able to discern the truth and attain self-awarness and sustainability? Is this all part of a great divine plan that is scripted with each of its unique characters that reinforce a MATRIX reality that invites revolutionizing and escaping? Do we ultimately hold all the keys to all back-doors into our sovereign spiritual freedom? After reading this material it should be fairly easy to form educated opinion or belief for yourself.*

The Gnostic creation of Adam and Eve is a story that also has quite a different twist in the Gnostic version than what has become almost completely accepted in today's society. The Chief Ruler, Yaldabaoth and his son, Sabaoth, expanded their creation to include beings of all sorts; these beings became the rulers of their vast creations. As time cycled on, the father and son team (Rulers) became proficient at fashioning great genetic creatures, both males and females, who did have the ability to procreate, but still without the pure essence of spirit. At some point the original offspring, the "*Children of the Children of Light*" of the Co-Creators, became interested in the nature of the materially created creatures. They conversed among themselves and decided to go down for a closer look and as they pressed down into that lower dimension to get a better look, their reflections were seen on the water of matter, so to speak.

These creation stories conclude that Sabaoth and his rulers were deeply impacted by seeing the reflections of the perfect humans from above. This caused the rulers to become enamored and infatuated with them. Sabaoth wanted to capture them and interact with them, so Sabaoth made inanimate forms after their image and likeness, both male and female, to attract them. However, these bodies where not capable of movement, as they lay lifeless on the earth, but with full consciousness, as consciousness exists in everything, rock and clay alike. This greatly interested Zoe (meaning Life/Breath), the Daughter of Sophia, who took pity on the modeled form and sent out a spark of her light essence to the female form. This light entered Eve and raised her up making her fully *alive.* Eve then blew a breath of her *Spirit* into Adam and gave him life in this manner.

The trap had succeeded to capture the essence of the perfect human beings into matter. Eventually the rulers became very angry and jealous because they saw that these beings were smarter and more powerfully present than themselves, giving them greater abilities and wisdom. Even though they where not fully aware of all their genius.

The Rulers tried to keep their 'creations' contained in their garden, telling them not to eat of the tree of Good and Evil. For this would reveal the truth about the Rulers and their ways. However, Sophia and Sanat Kumara were watching all that was going on, also took pity and decided to intervened by having Sophia appear as a snake in the tree, telling Eve to eat and learn the truth. Of course, they were then cast out of the garden. Before that the rulers raped Eve and she gave birth to twins, this boy and girl would be the generations of the "corrupted race"; the Canaanites after Cain. Sophia's twin counterpart (Sanat Kumara) wished to assist in the ensuing situation, so he '*came*' to Zoe/Eve, creating the first physical Immaculate Conception; a son called Seth. Who would be the seed of the true divine perfect human race on Earth.

Many struggles came from this attempt at infusing spirit into matter. The rulers would continue to try to defile the woman of the "incorruptible race". In some cases, they succeeded, bringing into existence giants and unusual creatures. Sabaoth and the rulers reached a point where they were so upset at the intervention of the invisible creator beings that they decided to cause a flood that would wipe out the perfect race and leave the generations of Noah (Canaanites) safe within an ark. The invisible Eternals who now had many of their offspring incarnating into the material drama experience, would not let such a tragedy happen to their children. Therefore, they gathered them together in "a great luminous cloud, which descended upon them."

When the waters had receded they were returned to earth. As time went on the incorruptible, immovable great race of Seth, became influenced and confused, losing the understanding of who they truly were. It is interesting to note here how this story could have ended up reading like what we find in the bible. Where we basically have the exact opposite of the truth as it was turned around to hide the truth about the "God of Israel", who is Sabaoth, which has been transliterated into Satan (from the Greek word *thetan* or "*thinker*") and the Elohim (or the sons of

Heaven) who were the *rulers*, the progenitors of Adam and Eve's earthly form. No wonder the Gnostics were the number one adversary persecuted by the early church fathers.

It is also very interesting to note that the Bible's word Elohim is translated to mean: Creators, a word in plural form. How could this be? The Bible states that God said, "I am the *one* Most High God and there are no others before me." As you may now begin to see this could have been the most seditious form of lies and tactics for suppressing and deceiving the perfect human race of beings from their true birthright. Naturally, everything serves its purpose in the divine plan of soul evolution. The cosmic scales have been out of balance for a very long time. Although now with the nearing of completion of the greatest experiment at hand, many souls are remembering their divine heritage and beginning to choose to take up the journey home. However, many other reminders, from Christ Conscious infusions to full embodiments of the *12 of the 24* have been necessary to begin to shake awake the slumbering masses.

What is being presented here for our consideration is the strong possibility that the Roman Catholic Church, which is the oldest corporation and political machine in the late world, may have been setup for taking over the world, as we shall see in more detail as we proceed. The Emperors, Rulers and Popes and Bishops were all very aware of the secrets to supreme power, which had as its foundation and main ingredient; the Goddess or more importantly, as we shall also see, the perfect balance of male and female polarities.

This is one of the main reasons the Roman Church so desperately wanted to silence the Gnostics, as they taught the importance of the female essence. In fact, they had within their practice or ceremony of mass, women equally giving sermons at the pulpit. The Church was out raged over this, eventually declaring a religious war against the Gnostics, attempting to cut the *EVIL* off at its roots.

After reviewing the entire body of this overwhelming wealth of material, evidenced within these pages, it is my strong belief and hope that you will come to agree with what is being portrayed here as the most closely preserved story of the essence of creation and the suppression of the Goddess. This knowledge coupled with self-mastery, resulted in the denouncing of the Gnostics as heretics, as more than mere conjecture.

*"The Rulers thought that it was by their own power and will that they did what they did. But the Holy Spirit was secretly activating the entirety through them, as it willed." ~ Gospel of Phillip*

## The Early Church Fathers
*(Neo-History)*

*What happens when you give absolute power to one body, be it a government or religion? Let alone both in under one roof. Can any say absolute corruption?*

It would be appropriate at this time to bring to the light, so to speak, possibly one of the oldest conspiracies known to humanity. If you do your spiritual due diligence surrounding the history of the earliest known records of Christianity and the Church, what you will find will amaze you and most likely shock you. The church and God in the name of religion have single-handedly been the most compromising obstruction to humanities fullest awakening and Self-Realization.

Down through the ages many attempts have been made to reawaken humanity and with every new approach or infusion of light there would always be a countering measure by the Lucifer Rebellion or opposing forces, call them what you may (albeit in perfection). Probably, the most powerful and ironic of them all is the long-lived Christianity or Churchianity. Some people would find this most absurd, as well as extremely offensive. Although, when you really do your homework, all the proof is there in the history of their records: the scriptures. The shear amount of information available is rather astounding, as we shall discover.

From the Gnostic Scriptures, to the Dead Sea scrolls, to the Pseudepigrapha, to the Jewish Mystics, and to the Christian Apocrypha (Hidden Books or Secret Books Because these secret books were often preserved for use within the esoteric circles of the divinely - knit believers, many of the critically - spirited or "unenlightened" Church Fathers found themselves outside the realm of understanding, and therefore came to apply the term "apocryphal" to, what they claimed to be, heretical works which were forbidden to be read.), these are the more commonly known works previously accepted. Until the early Church Fathers at Constantinople in 381 AD, choose which books to include in the Bible, from the myriad of all existing scriptures at the time. They chose the preferred ones that would make up the sole *"Word of God"*, or the authorized and accepted beliefs, while anathematizing the rest along with their authors. (The process of homogenization and propagation had been under way for at least a century considering Lucius Domitius Aurelian, a Roman emperor who ruled from 270-275

AD, burned the Royal Quarter of the Alexandrian Library.) The Roman Church Fathers ultimately choose the best scriptures that best fit their agenda, only to make minor additions to those, which were close enough to the mark for their deception. From several hundred works (and several thousand in the Alexandrian Library) to choose from, they ended up with just a few dozen hand picked scriptures to support their propaganda. Even the most accepted and widely used by the first followers of Jesus where rejected, namely the *Gospel of Barnabas*. It is interesting to note that they were in control of the infamous literary wealth of the Alexandrian Library in Egypt, which mysteriously burned not to long afterwards for the second time, since Cleopatra's death and the loss of Egypt's heritage and sovereignty in 50 BC.

As you really study the entire body of work surrounding God or Yahweh and Jesus the Nazarene, the truth becomes very obvious and blatant. This was a truth that as a young man of 16, I knew the Roman Catholic Church was not telling me the whole story. Therefore, once I became an adult at 18 I left the church to try to find what I knew as truth in my own heart and soul. My Quest was very guided by Spirit, filled with synchronicities and miracles, as I confirmed what I innately knew. My quest was not purely a desire to debauch the Church, but to answer personal questions about my origin and inner truths, which was of a very pure spiritual nature.

What I found will astonish some and invigorate others, for example, reincarnation was an accepted fact in the early Gnostic Christians belief system and was actually taught and kept alive outside of the controlling aspect of the Vatican well into the 17th Century. For example, the following from the book entitled Pistis Sophia.

*The Virgin of Light (Mother Sophia) tests the soul and when she has discerned the nature of its sins (lessons and growth) and whether it has stood upright, she will cast a part of her light-power (essence) into it, because of the body and the community of senses, which I have explained to you in the expansion of the universe. The Virgin of Light then seals that soul and hands it over to one of her Receivers to have it cast into a suitable body, depending upon which sins it has committed. I tell you the truth; they will not permit that soul to escape the changes of the body (cycle of reincarnation) until it has completed its last circuit, according to its merit.*

Although probably the most profound truth concealed behind blood stained lies, for the sake of controlling the masses and manipulating the wealthy, was the vital truth and knowledge about who we truly are. This had to be hidden at whatever the cost. If the Truth was released everyone would be empowered with the knowledge of who and what they truly are and could not be controlled. It is rather unsettling to comprehend the ruthlessness of the early Church Fathers, who could have coined the phrase, "if you cannot beat 'em, join 'em". Because when the Gnostic and Essene sects, who were the true follows of Christ, only labeled by the Romans as Christians, were at there strongest, the Emperor basically said, whoever is a Christian is an enemy of the state and shall be put to death. Once they saw the strength of conviction and determination of the followers of Christ, they decided to use it to their own advantage, and created a new Religion, where the edict was, "One God, One Ruler". So now, the law required the reverse of the previous fate. Become a 'Roman Christian' or face death. They also modified the Gnostic statement, *"Jesus Christ, the first begotten Son of God"* to "Jesus Christ the one and only begotten Son of God."

Additionally there was another sect flourishing at the time; the Pagans, men and women who held the sacred truths about the gods, goddess, elementals, divas and fairies, which by the way were the previous choices of the Romans. The High Priestess of this order at that time was Mary Magdalene. Yes, she was hated by the Church Fathers for many more reasons than the bible ever hinted at. She was resurrecting the ancient ways of living in harmony and balance with the Earth and one another. She was the embodiment of the essence of the Divine Mother of Ancient Egypt, representing the *"Return of the Goddess"* movement, which had been reinstated many times down through the ages. A few of the most noteworthy were the female Egyptian Pharaoh; Hat-sept-sut and Nefertiti.

The Roman Catholic Church would actually break their own precise laws of Moses to attempt to manipulate the Pagans into their lair, by erecting statues of Mother Mary in the Church in an effort to say, "There is your Goddess, the Mother of All, come worship her in our Temple." This would be in direct violation of the commandment, *"Thou shall not have any graven images, the similitude of any figure, the likeness of male or female, beast, winged fowl, fish or any thing that creepeth on the ground."* Yet there she stood in all her glory. How deep would the blasphemy and travesties run?

It was at this time when women were more severely suppressed than ever before. Because it was known that if women were allowed to know their true empowerments, their inherent unabridged love and power would be a great force to reckon with. Moreover, one-half of the divine equation would be complete.

The understanding of what really was going on starts with the truth about the "God of Israel", who was a real being that interacted with the people at that time. He was not God in the Highest, but a demiurge or "half maker" (a watered down form of a co-creator). This being or god was a jealous god; this god was feared and wanted it that way for power and control. It would not have any other beings exercising their free will as divine co-creators as long as it was around. The statement made by Jesus bares exceptional credence here, *"Do you not know that ye too are gods?"* and *"Ye shall do greater things than I"*, as the true Children of the Light that you are.

This Ruler "god" would wipe out an entire tribe or generation for mere disobedience alone. This god went by the name of Yahweh or Yaldabaoth, for here we see the return of the Chief Ruler from the Garden. This god demanded that he be feared and worshiped. He was known for the commandment, *"you shall worship me and have no other gods before me"*. If he were truly the highest God, what concern would he have of others before him, for nothing exists above or beyond the infinite Creator? Jesus was even known to refer to the Israelites god, as their God or 'your god', versus his references to my Father (God the Highest) who is in Heaven. This surely was not some jealous being that lived in a tent in the middle of the desert.

I know full well that my Creator is a God of Love, not some monster that would innocently slay an entire generation of people because the head priest burned the wrong incense at the wrong offering time. There are many other travesties far too many to name here. (Some references are: Numbers 11:31-33, 16:15-33, 16:41-50). Check your Bible, and discern who your God truly is. It is time to reclaim your power, stop the dis-empowering Churchianity, and take our beloved Brother Jesus off the cross, which is nothing more than another form of idol worship in and of itself. My Creator is a God who welcomes you to pray in private, behind close doors in secret and total communion, one on one, in whatever way you are comfortable with. Many things begin to stand out when you look at the Bible in this new light. It has been written that the Old and New Testament do not actually belong together in the same book. (i.e. The Gospel of Marcion.)

The New Testament also has many words of disinformation as well. Although I would also like to state that, I do believe there are many good inspirational words in the bible, which truly are a reflection of the beauty and divinity of the human spirit. It is up to you and your own heart as a truth filter to discern where you are giving away your power and rights as a sovereign divine being. Therefore, this is where the tale really begins. Now that we have set the stage, let the *"Greatest Story Never Told"* unfold in hopes of freeing your soul to fly to the heights of the Eternal Realm.

It would behoove those who are having trouble with the text written on these pages to take this opportunity to really listen and truly weigh the words within your own heart. It absolutely knows the full truth when it hears it. It is your personal guide and truth filter and will resonate and attune to the TRUTH when it is given in unconditional love. A very good reputed Christian source for more information about the Gnostics is by Dr. Elaine Pagels in the book entitled, "The Gnostic Gospels". She does an exceptional job of amassing all the best statements by the Gnostic Apostles and sheds some light on the possibility of a greater truth and remain investigative with a open mind. Although at best is only scratching the surface of the true esoteric nature of the order. In order to delve into the next layers one must let go of the need for purely mental pursuits and truly listen and look for the language of the heart. Many things within the Bible are left to interpretation and it is the intention of the insight that is gained, which is most liberating and rewarding. Forcing interpretation on anyone is nothing less than control[5].

---

[5] The Roman Catholic Church declared itself the only authority to interpret the Holy Scripture at the Council of Trent in 1546:-

*... no one relying on his own judgment and distorting the Sacred Scriptures according to his own conception shall dare to interpret them contrary to that sense which Holy Mother Church, to whom it belongs to judge their true sense and meaning, has held or does hold, or even to interpret them contrary to the unanimous agreement of the Fathers.*

Some suffered the ultimate penalty at the hands of the Catholic Church for their beliefs. Giordano Bruno, in *Cena de le Ceneri* (1584), declared his support for the reality of the heliocentric theory and also claimed that the universe is infinite. Bruno's works where related to Metaphysics and Mathematics. In this work he also argued that the Holy Scripture was written to teach morals but not to teach astronomy. It is a little difficult to know exactly what he was accused of during his seven year trial. Bruno seems not to have understood himself for when the Inquisition demanded that he retract, he replied that he had nothing to retract and did not understand what he was being asked to retract. Giordano Bruno was sentenced to death by the Inquisition and burned alive in February 1600.

How many centuries of senseless slaughter must humanity endure in the name of God, Church and Redemption? To this brutal end our beloved soul sister; Joan of Ark! Today's chastising of everyone as sinners is just as senseless of a behavior. Jesus did not die on the cross for our sins. We are not sinners from birth. We chose the LIGHT and left the Garden. Needing a Savior is dis-empowering to the truth of who and what we really are. It is only ourselves that can and must, realize our true heritage, and claim our own *AT-ONE-MENT*.

I invite you to drink from the pure spiritual streams of Truth that Jesus taught directly to the Apostles, which have been recorded in earnest as the *Gnostic Scriptures*. This is the truth as I remember it and as Spirit has led me to find and in some cases decode. The inner teachings of the mystery schools were guarded with life itself and encrypted to prevent the profane from misusing the wisdom or *throwing pearls in the mud*, as Jesus would say. This wisdom is returning now for these are truly the end days when, *"All things shall be revealed"*.

Here is further evidence of what Jesus was dealing with in the days of his early ministry, before the disciples where initiated into Apostles.

> *"Simon Peter said, 'Mary Magdalene should leave us, for females are not worthy of life!' Jesus said, 'See here, I am going to attract her to make her male, so that she too might become a living spirit that resembles you males. For every woman that makes herself male will enter the Kingdom of Heaven."* ~ *Gospel of Thomas*

The above statement makes it very clear that in the first years of the gathering of the disciples that they did not yet have ears to hear. The social conditioning of the times still had a very tight grasp on their minds. It would be sometime before Jesus would actually be able to teach them the mysteries of heaven without parables and allegories. If he would have said you will also need to balance your female aspect, before gaining their trust they would have thought that he was crazy. Jesus later teaches the full truth of the need to fully balance both energies as one, as we shall see.

Within these pages, there will be revealed startling evidence that the ancients knew that the key to everything lies in the profound statement that *"the Two must become One"*.

THE 7TH SEAL

Probably the most controversial or contradictory subject in the bible is the significance of Satan and yet there are very few references to who and what he really is. There are several references to a particular enigmatic phrase that interpretation has dictated to be Satan or Lucifer.

The second part of this book will fully elucidated the truth about the mysterious title and role of the "Morning Star".

The following examples demonstrate a grave contradiction in the eyes of Christians today who try to read the Bible word for word, taking the dead letter as the living Spirit.

When in reality it is a key to the door to everlasting life!

The Old Testament calls the fallen creature of Isaiah 14:12 "Morning Star".

"I, (Jesus), have sent my angel to give you [1] this testimony for the churches. I am the Root and the Offspring of David, and the bright Morning Star." ~ Revelation 22:16

"And we have the word of the prophets made more certain, and you will do well to pay attention to it, as to a light shining in a dark place, **until the day dawns and the morning star rises in your hearts**." ~ 2 Peter 1:19

"I will also give him the morning star." ~ Revelation 2:28

All in all, this boldly states that Lucifer and Jesus are ONE!

I have seen many contradictions in the Bible; however this one is the most intriguing and when analyzed thoroughly reveals great insight or Gnosis.

This subject will be fully explained and demonstrated in the chapter entitled "Divine Atomic Energy" and "The Lock and the Key"

Remember, what is being laid out here in part one are the foundational understandings that setup the various premises for the unveiling of the Hidden Wisdom in the Greater Mysteries. The relationship to the morning star and stars in general will also be covered in numerous ways as well. What will become fairly obvious is the tactic if you want to hide something important place it in plain view and simply change the perception of it. Namely call it EVIL and off limits for fear of damnation.

Furthermore, there is a comprehensive system of numbers that underpins all these references and ideologies. Multiple ciphers have been created to hide the whole truth. When one has all the keys to the kingdom, so to speak, all things are revealed!

THE 7TH SEAL

## Remember, Behold Seth's Great Race
### (Neo-History)

*If this is indeed a grand play focused on the world stage, who are the leading stars and what are their roles? Have they always played their parts the same or do they change teams or sides as well? Or is this like almost everything else; a matter of perception? If so, where do the boundaries lay and who placed them and better yet; can they be broken. And if so, what will it take to do so, is it accomplished by one or many?* ⚕

Seth was the third son of Adam and Eve, well sort of, according to the bible anyway. He was actually more significant than that, for he was the first incarnation of the male aspect of the 12 Ray Divine Twinships child, the brother of our beloved Zoe (the son of Sanat Kumara: El Morya, see page 71 for deeper description). These would have also been the first oversouls to project sparks of themselves as the production of souls for inhabiting material bodies. In other words, their offspring in the invisible realm would begin to come down and inhabit this gross material plane. Accordingly as we have learned, Zoe (again, the daughter of Sophia and Santa Kumara) was the first infusion of spirit to animate Adam and Eve, would remain to this day as a guiding motherly spiritual figure that is woven into many incarnate Goddess women, as in the consciousness of this greater aspect is awakened.

At some point according to the Gnostics, Eve's second son Cain kills his brother Abel out of lust and jealousy for his sister, who is his twin and mate. (We will discover profound direct correlations to the Egyptians and their cosmology later regarding this very story!) This by the way was a trait they say passed down to Cain by his true father, Sabaoth, son of Yaldabaoth. For remember he raped Eve and the outcome was Cain, and Abel's father was Yaldabaoth, whose offspring were the race of the Giants. "This is the whole story behind the one verse in the biblical account of; "That the sons of god, saw the daughters of men, that they were fair, and they took to them all they chose." In addition, "there were giants in the earth in those days, when the sons of god came unto the daughters of men, and they bare children to them, the same became mighty men of old, men of renown. " ~*Genesis 6:4.* The beings are called the Nephilim or Nephelas (those who come on clouds) or the Watchers from the Bible and various versions of the Secret Book of Enoch, their chief ruler is Samyaza. There are many references to clouds, entering and exiting, as well as one that talks about the return of a Christed One.

Therefore, when Abel was murdered it became an opportunity to interject or intervene with a race that was truly fashioned after the divine perfect human, not just in image, but also in Soul and Spirit. So an immaculate conception was setup for Eve, who would give birth to the twin soul of Sophia and Santa Kumara. This twin birth is where the first occurrence of the title "son of man" comes from; these are the children of the Perfect Human Beings. The Gnostic Scriptures refer to this as the Child of the Child, the Twin Savior (Children of the parents who are children of the first parent entity).

Some Gnostics postulated that this was the first incarnation of Jesus; I do not necessarily believe that is exactly the case, yes it would have been an incarnation of a Christ being. Remember the First Begotten Son/Daughter twins, (*not the only begotten as Churchianity has it*), was the being who is Jesus (Sananda Kumara) and the Last begotten twins where Sanat Kumara and Sophia, who were in a sense responsible for the creation of Yaldabaoth and his creations. So hence, they felt responsible to assist as much as possible. After all, that was their daughter down there, and soon to be two children (El Morya and Zoe) who would then be the first King and Queen of the earthly dominion.

This now introduced a new twist to the stage or perhaps stacked deck. Enter; the Great Race of Seth. Seth means the *"one who was sent"*. This race of beings was very well balanced and still very connected to their inner truth and knowing. This may well have been the root of the race and civilization known as the Lemurians. These beings lived in harmony and peace for quite some time. Although they did have some troubles periodically with the Giant race.

**[It is also most significant to understand that Seth has been called to Father of Astrology/Astronomy. Some 30 years later, after great urging by my Higher Self and research the importance of the Zodiac story or the Gospel in the Stars is clearly understood. I had strong insights underlining the significance early on, but didn't have all the data. Now there is a complete story that was a thread when I began this journey]**

After some time had passed a great war would arise, with the Giants most likely desiring more land, woman and possessions. This was a terrible war indeed, with tremendous death and destruction, with the inevitable set back and loss of great progress in soul development. It was decided that an attempt would be made to minimize the damage of such karma and desolation. So the decision was made to send down a direct manifestation of the parent entity, the father of El Morya and Zoe, *Sanat Kumara*; *"The Ancient of Days."* (Sanathana = Ancient and also eternal and Kumara = Kuma Ra =Guardian of the Divine Fire) Sanat Kumara actually figures into several roles in the religious traditions of the East. Each one reveals another facet of his Divine Self. In each role, he teaches us something different about the Creator and about our path to Source.

Sanat Kumara is revered in Hinduism as one of the seven sons of Brahma. They are portrayed as youths who have remained pure. The Sanskrit name Sanat Kumara means "*always a youth.*" In Hinduism, Sanat Kumara is sometimes called Skanda, or Karttikeya the son of Shiva and Parvati. Karttikeya is the god of war and commander-in-chief of the gods. He is the commander and chief of the divine army of the gods (*interesting correlation to his son Yaldabaoth*). He was born specifically to slay Táraka, the demon who symbolizes ignorance, or the lower mind. Karttikeya is often depicted holding a spear, this spear represents illumination. He uses the spear to slay ignorance.

In Hinduism, stories of war are often used as allegories for the internal struggles of the soul. Indian author A. Parthasarathy says that Karttikeya represents the *"Man of Perfection who has discovered the Supreme Self"*. The wielding of his spear of annihilation symbolizes the destruction of all negative tendencies which veil the Divine Self." This is also true of many of the Egyptian wall art portraying the slaying of enemies. Schwaller De Lubicz emphasizes this in his extensive studies of the Nile temples. Let alone that the Gemini Twins carry spears!

Skanda-Karttikeya, as he is sometimes called, is also acclaimed as the god of wisdom and learning. He is said to bestow spiritual powers upon his devotees, especially the power of knowledge. An inscription on a fifth-century stone pillar in Northern India describes Skanda as the guardian of the Divine Mothers.

> *The Divine Mother is in you. Her abiding place, as you know, is the white four-pedaled chakra at the base of the spine. This sacred fire is your life force. It is the energy that rises to meet the light that descends over the crystal cord. You can see the crystal cord on the Chart of the Presence. The energy of the Father-Mother God descends over the crystal cord and the sacred fire of the Mother rises from the*

THE 7TH SEAL

*base chakra. So, we are nourished by Father above and by Mother below and yet Father above contains Mother, and Mother below contains Father."*

In southern India, Karttikeya is known by the name of Subramanya, which means "dear to the Brahmans;" the members of the priestly caste. Every village, even the smallest, has a temple or shrine to Subramanya.

In the Hindu mystic tradition, Karttikeya is known as Guha, which means "cave" or Secret One, because he lives in the cave of your heart. How secure we must feel knowing that the Lord Sanat Kumara, the Great Guru who sponsors earth, her evolutions and all Buddhas and Bodhisattvas and Christed Ones actually lives in the cave of our heart?

Hindu scriptures also depict Sanat Kumara as the "foremost of sages" and a knower of Brahman. The Ascended Masters teach that the supreme God of Zoroastrianism, Ahura Mazda, is *Sanat Kumara*. Ahura Mazda means "Wise Lord" or "Lord who bestows intelligence."

In Summary, Sanat Kumara is the dispeller of ignorance. He represents the principle of Good and is the guardian of mankind. This relates with much of the Channeled information that talks about how Sanat Kumara at earths darkest hour, held the earth and its inhabitants in his blue ray for protection. The story of this war was also passed down in history and survives today in the East Indian tradition as the Avatar Krishna's entrance into the world to help in the Great War. After the war, it is said that Krishna's twin and bride joined him in celebration of the peace. The story follows that what additionally happened is Krishna's (Sanat Kumara's) twin became the embodiment of the planetary logos, Earth Mother Gaia (Pistis Sophia). This added a great balance of as above, so below or making the inside like the outside, or perhaps literally connecting the top with the bottom. From this time forward, the Earth was truly alive and all of existence was cradled in love and light from above to below. It is interesting to note that Job in the Old Testament said, *"Speak to the Earth, and she will teach you."* This does not seem like the kind of thing you would find in the Old Testament, considering what we now know. The best way to deceive is to interlace and disperse truth among dis-information.

The Gnostic Scriptures say that, *"Christ came to rectify the separation that had been present since the beginning and to join the two components and to give eternal life to those who had died by separation."* ~ Gospel of Thomas

*"Frequently there descends He who is blessed forever."* ~ Book of Enoch 76:2

# Cosmology of the Geometric Twinships
### (Neo-History)

*Regardless of whether or not anyone is watching the movie on the big screen in the sky, the cosmic clock still ticks off its minutes within every human heart. This grand play or divine plan has a definite beginning and ending act. We are in the eleventh hour and the team in the halo's are 5 yards from a touch down, we are behind in points and yet the underdog will win because it is through the spirit and emotional excitement that the most impact is made causing the whole stadium to stand up and cheer "GOOD GAME"! Oh, and everyone loves a good mystery.*

So now then, we now have the story line of the creation myth with Adam and Eve representing the infusion or projection of souls into matter for the experiences of expression in an individualized or externalized form. From the Metaphysical aspect of this story, it represents the unfolding of the ONE consciousness into a myriad of selves, discovering Self; or the ultimate 'Collective Whole'. For in the beginning when the "Creator Beings", the host of Eternal Divine Twins, began creating projections or reflections of themselves, which are the first cause 'monads' or Children of Light, i.e. "sons of man", or more appropriately the sons and daughters of the Perfect Divine Human Beings. Their race or offspring are called, "the Generation over whom there is no kingdom" or the *"immovable race"*; this is the *"Kingdom of Light"* or simply pure spirit.

These beings were also a form of creator beings; they are referred to as the 'Co-Creators'. These twin sister/brother children each created an entity or projection of themselves, which was outside of the realm of the second principle or the kingdom of light. This is when the creation of the 'Oversouls', first occurred, this is also known as when the *'invisible became visible'*. We find references to this in some of the iterations of the Gnostic texts as the Adam and Eve story. The oversouls where set up to be the storehouses of all the experiences, as a unique identity, which would grow, and evolve based on its experiences throughout all of creation.

When a certain level of growth was attained through self-awareness and realization of whom self truly was (is), one would under go the process of ascension back to the realm of the Children of Light or the Eternal Realm. The oversoul was endowed with the ability to further create or again project aspects of itself into matter and various planes of existence to accumulated experiences and wisdom. These aspects of self are the souls, which embody all of the sentient life forms of creation, and in some cases the animal kingdom and nature kingdom within the entire universe. The oversoul still maintained the original blueprint of the male and female aspect of the respective progenitor pair, as well as the essence of that divine couple's parents, the divine first begotten twins. This is the representation of the 12 rays of creation and their respective quality and characteristics reflected down, essentially fractured through the dimensions as lineage, or as relations such as what became the 12 tribes of Israel. Again, this is the same energetic emulation of the 12 houses of the Zodiac.

The process of oversoul transformation, which is the return or absorbing of the soul from the incarnating experience, also occurs in respect to its origin. In other words, the female aspect would return to its originating female aspect of the oversoul. Likewise for the male aspect, for the oversoul always followed suite with the male/female bisecting pattern set by the original, first gotten son/daughter Twinships. This fractalizing quality, again directly follows the Fibonacci and Phi principle. The term "Twin Flames" comes from the male and female aspect of oversoul in full soul expression interacting with direct relation to one another. Moreover, the term "Soul Mates", actually means souls who have essentially become friends, or who have embodied and encounter one another many times agreeing to assist one another in their spiritual evolution. This soul grouping has also been called soul families, which generally run up in line with the ray or lineage. There are also lesser degrees of intensity of connection as the reference moves out into the other areas that represent soul family alignment. These are the adjacent houses and the one directly across from the reference point on the zodiacal wheel, known as an opposition. These interactions often create the best opportunities for the greatest growth.

Therefore, the actual Twin Flame incarnations and interactions have been more rare and when agreed upon are usually such incarnations as to make a strong impact in the realms of experiences and lessons for greater collective soul growth. Literally, the unfolding of the divine plan, for naturally there is a greater service that can be rendered when the power of the same soul is combined. More and more the occurrence of Twin Flames has been setting the stage for an intricate piece in the plan of the returning to source. As the oversoul reaches its required level of evolution, the oversoul would return to its previous state, which is known as the 'Oversoul Transformation'.

This process could occur independent of the growth or evolution of the opposite respective oversouls aspect. Namely, the Ascension at this level did not require the completion of the counterparts' respective male/female aspect. For example in the case of the female, lets say she was to graduate to an Ascended Master, she would not have to wait for her male counterpart to move to the next level of reuniting with her Co-Creating aspect in the Eternal Realm. Nevertheless, she would have to wait at this level to return or reunite to the next level of Divine Twinships; the third level, beneath the parent entities, naturally assisting her compliment. This hold up is due to the requirement of the reunification into the whole as one reunited entity in a balanced process, as it is necessary to roll up or return in the same manner or pattern as the unfolding originally took place by.

To this date the full reunification of the Children of Light with the Divine Twins has not occurred, although this is one of the changes that will begin taking place with the Shift, and ever the more so. Again, more on these deeper cosmological levels later, we must first fully cement a substantial foundation to ground and align your souls light more directly with its own oversoul. Therefore, to summarize, the souls evolve back into the oversouls and the oversouls evolve or return to the Co-Creating, Children of Light, monad; as Ascended Masters. It is again noteworthy to mention that the Angels _are_ the Children of Light, which represent the higher form of the human being, in other words the *perfect human*, hence the wings on beautiful androgynous *perfect humans*, depicting beings that can soar to great heights.

Jesus said, "I will give to you the Keys to the Kingdom of Heaven; and whatever you bind on earth will have been bound in heaven, and whatever you loose on earth will have been loosed in heaven. And if <u>two of you</u> on earth shall agree about anything, you will ask for it and it shall be done for you by my Father who is in heaven." ~ Gospel of Matthew

# Melchizedek Dispensation
### (Neo-History)

*Every good action adventure needs it hero, who is selfless and diligently driven. The script would be out of balance and not effective if it didn't have a supporting cast and a leading lady. This group of stars is a little harder to discern against the backdrop of a night sky filled with extras and props that make the entire deliverance possible. Never the less the plot is reinforced throughout all the sequels that come rolling out over time.*

When the Great Race of Seth was beginning to flourish, again it was decided by the Council of the Eternals that the time had come to introduce the Melchizedek Order of Ascended Teachers. The dispensation would begin to harvest the souls who where ready to under go the Ascension process, the first mystery school was established and the dissemination of the knowledge required to attain the required level of spiritual awareness began.

The Melchizedek dispensation would serve several purposes, leadership, consultation and education, as well as holding the balance of love, the essence and frequency of the Great Spirit. This was to ensure that the force of love would be present, as the force of the Mind/Soul aspect was overbearingly strong due to the manifested presence of Sabaoth. This balance was crucial to maintaining a harmony of the polarities, since this was a free will zone, which had been set up to experience individual choice in a duality consciousness.

It became necessary to ensure that a clear choice was present, although ultimately the Gnosis is that one must be in balance with the entire mind/body system. For the complete make up of the perfect human has the energy fields of all the bodies' components in balance, the Merkaba (light-body) comprises all the dynamics of this total divine composition. This is the way the full embodiment of a Christ conscious being was accomplished. Through the use of the Merkaba, this maintained the integrity of the true self's awareness, as this is the basis for the return to that awareness as well. The first Melchizedek being was the actual spiritual Father of Seth's soul.

This was the Eternal Being who was responsible for the creation of the material kingdom or visible realm through the Yaldabaoth being, so it was his son who volunteered to make the first real concerted effort and appearance. This is the Ascended Master El Morya, who to this day is the Ascended Master who brought the Great White Brotherhood to earth. Over the course of Earth's history four other Melchizedek beings would come to serve in the capacity of divine liaison for human kind from the Realm of Eternal Light.

Many other incarnations of Christ conscious beings would grace the earth through figures such as; Buddha, Zoroaster, Enoch, Osiris and Jesus. There are also the presences of magnanimous Goddesses who reinforce the leading men, they will be introduced to the rest of the cast in part two. When Jesus was incarnate, he was called a High Priest after the Order of Melchizedek. (Hebrews, chapter 5) The Old Testament again has some accurate information when it makes these types of statements about Melchizedek, stating, *"He was born without father or mother and without beginning or end."* When Abraham encountered Melchizedek, he offered bread and wine to Abraham in a ceremony, where Abraham recognized him as the High Priest and King of Salem (King of Righteousness or King of Peace.) This is also a reference to the earliest Egyptian civilization (known as Khem) in 28,000 B.C, when the first Avatar/Melchizedek incarnation was El Morya as Hr; the first Pharaoh.

The Gnostic Scriptures have this to say, *"Melchizedek is parlamentor of the light, and purifier of the light."* The word parlamentor doesn't exist in our language today, the closest is parliament, which is a legal body of government. The French word parler means to speak. They said he was of Immaculate Conception and a God incarnate, like the Son of God. Hence one of the Eternal Divine Twins fully incarnate! Pistis Sophia also states that Melchizedek is the Great Receiver of Light, who is in the region of the Right, who will seal the soul, as well as can all his Receivers and they will lead the purified soul into the Treasury of Light.

The first mystery school setup by El Morya was the medium through which the very first ascension was accomplished; this is known as the resurrection of Osiris. Many channelings confirm that El Morya was one of the first ones to come to this plane and brought the Great White Brotherhood to assist.

El Morya is Chohan of the First Ray, the blue ray, of power, goodwill and faith. He also exemplifies the blue-ray qualities of leadership, proper use of power and speech, and ultimate surrender to the divine will. He can assist all students who desire to embody these virtues, master the throat chakra and receive the Holy Spirit's gifts of the word of wisdom and faith in the divine will.

El Morya is well known as the Master M who worked with the Master Koot Hoomi in the late nineteenth century to establish the Theosophical Society and to spread the knowledge of higher truths to a wider circle among mankind. After his ascension in the late 1800s, he continued working for this same purpose, most notably through Nicholas and Helena Roerich in the early 1900's and recently through The Summit Lighthouse and Mark and Elizabeth Prophet beginning in the late 1950s.

Some of El Morya's most important teachings concern the will of God, the divine will that lies within each of us. He explains that by aligning with and embracing this will one gradually becomes reunited with his own Higher Self. Following the divine will also leads to out picturing the inner blueprint of the soul and to fulfilling one's unique mission in life. El Morya and the blue-ray masters always teach that if the student's will is one with the will of God, he will succeed.

El Morya's etheric retreat is located over Darjeeling, India.

## El Morya

*Jesus said, "When you see one who was not born of woman, fall on your faces and worship. That is your Father"* ~ *Gospel of Thomas, saying # 15.*

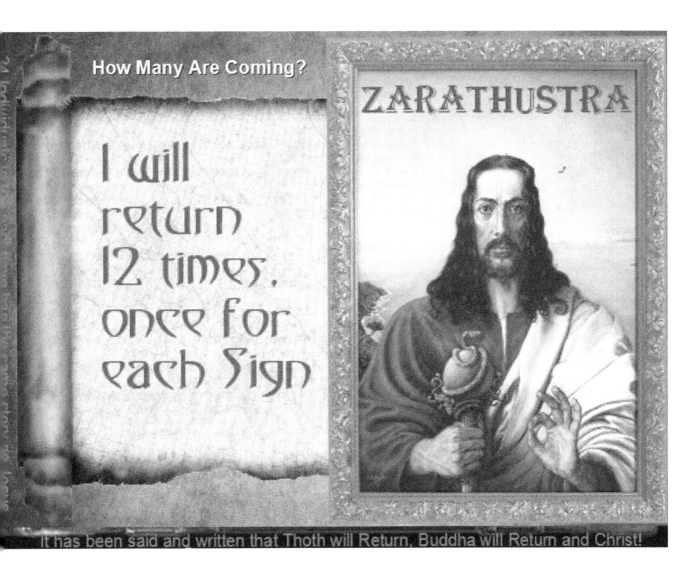

# Mystery Schools
(Gnosis /Neo-History)

*The organization, protection and deliverance of the learned wisdom were thought to be necessary due to the misuse by early civilizations. The creation of the Mystery School was done with great care and reverence for the body of material that could produce the most technically advanced and spiritually aware civilization that the face of the Earth has ever seen. The desire to rebuild Atlantis was at the heart of this intention, safeguarding against the shortcomings that lead to the collapse of this elder race and the loss of the history of our global heritage.*

The Mystery Schools that have come down through the ages have all been setup for the same reason, to teach the Truth and the Way. This is why Jesus said, *"I am the Truth and the Way and the Light."* The Truth is who you really are and where you really come from, and why you are really here. The Truth quite simply is 'Self-Realization', the knowing and understanding that you truly are God/Goddess. Each and everyone are the essence of the Creator and the soul's essence or Spirit Fragments of the Co-Creators. We are the fractalization or bifurcation of the Creator Beings. Each of us truly has a piece or reflection, so to speak, of the Creator within us, and this is the Spirit or Source Intelligence. We each have a pure and perfect connection to that source and its omnipresence consciousness, although it is up to us to have this realization in our own manner/reality. This is Self-Realization, when you finally get that great "ah-ha", "now I get it" and you really not only understand this fully but also become that awareness. It is each of our own personal choices to take this path and open to this truth.

THE 7TH SEAL

It does take some time to fully develop, although once you have gained the key and placed it within the lock on that inner door, Spirit will crack open that door. When and if you realize that it is still not opening and begin to knock, Spirit will show you more signs and light shinning through on how to fully open the door. The numbers are the most obvious signs! This is what lead me down my path when I was 17 years old.

The Way is the method or technique to accomplish this connection and the vehicle or way home; the Ascension. The vehicle is the Merkaba, the light body or *"Garment of Light"* that we put on to walk and travel interdimensionally on the highest path, the ultimate journey home. This is where the great reformation or reunification will occur, the complete return to our parents, our source, energetically reuniting in totality.

The Light is probably the most widely played upon metaphor or allegory in all of history, because it can literally be almost anything or used anywhere. It is truly consciously aware, and it is energy, as well as being the all-pervading information or intelligence of creation. It is simply omnipresent too and yet there is a significant difference between light and spirit, as we shall come to understand shortly. So follow the light, it will lead you home, and the light will show you your path along the way, and in truth it will also keep you company.

The main Mystery Schools we will focus on are the Egyptian, Pythagoras and the Gnostics. There has been many before these, such as the Melchizedek Order, which was circa 10,000 BC. There has been many civilizations on this planet for millions of years. We will be looking at ones that have a semblance of history that can been traced.

## The Egyptians

The greater part of this book will focus on the mysteries of the Egyptians who were the most refined as to the absolute truth of the ancient pure wisdom pertaining to the actual way to ascend, thus the allegory of the Resurrection of Osiris. After the pole shift and demise of Atlantis, the Ascended Masters, as the High Priests, reseeded the civilization in Egypt. The peak of the knowledge and wisdom was lost early on in Egyptian history probably at most within the first few thousand years. The civilization fell to a steady decline there after. Although the closest resurgence to the true understanding of the ancient wisdom was reached twice, once during the reign of King Zoser, when Imhotep arrived on the scene in circa 3000 BC, teaching the Egyptians to build pyramids. The first true Egyptian pyramid was setup at Saqqara, along with a mystery school about a mile south of the original instillation at Giza. The second time was in the 18th Dynasty (circa 1500 BC), with Amenhotep's generational line of aligned souls. These Kings had very strong connections to source and truth, namely; Hep-set-sutph, Tutmoses IV, Amenhotep III and Amenhotep IV, (Akhenaton). It was also a time when the most intellectual corruption of power and greed was seeping into the society, with a sect of priests and a very persuasive military faction leading the people astray from balance and harmony.

Therefore, it was decided to infuse a Christ Conscious being who would reinstate the Truths in a monumental way.[6] These leads us the emergence of Akhenaton a true divine Priest/King, along with the mystery school of all Mystery Schools. This school taught the old ways exactly as they where in the beginning, with the use of the Great Temple of Ascension, the largest Pyramid in Giza. We shall also discover another prominent *figure* that had his hands in assisting with the setting up of the mystery school and remained behind the scenes, surviving the systematically dismantling of this divine attempt to convert Egypt to the Forefather's old ways, the One Highest Creator and the Law of One, fully reinstate the ancient secret Order of the Melchizedeks.

Edgar Cayce the sleeping Prophet from the 1930's brought through vast amounts of information while he was in trance states, which helped many people with their aliments and general mind/body/spirit health. One of the side effects, as it were, was the past life information that came up surrounding the clients origins of disease. One of the origin dates that he brought through was in earliest Egyptian cultural settlements, which was 10,500 BC. Legends and his channeled material

---

[6] *There where other times in which the full glory of the divine was present in the Nile valley, although this was when the land was called Khem, which means the black land because of the rich soil created when the Nile was flooding annually. The presence of the da vince cadre walked with the people, the Khemurians, in circa 28,000 BC and again in 10,500 when the great pyramids where the central focus.*

states that the original designers and developers of Khem as; Thoth, Hept-Seph, and Ra/Osiris. We will discover a great deal more about these three characters and their full identities throughout this book and material.

Akhenaton was successful in assisting in the ascension of 300 beings, most of whom were women. This could be one of several reasons why so many women have been already waking up for some time now in this re-emergence of the Self-Realized Movement. In addition to the obvious, it is the "Return of the Goddess". There was a great deal of digging going on in the 30's due to Cayce's information. The tunnels under the Giza Plateau where found at that time, including a bust of Nefertiti in the tunnel leading from the Sphinx to the Great Pyramid, confirming the knowledge and use of the complex for initiation. Confirming what is being revealed here, that this Mystery School was using the original initiations techniques involving the Sphinx and Great Pyramid for the Ascension rite. Ascension was synonymous with Eternal life.

*Akhenaton*

The Ankh is defined as: The symbolic representation of both Physical and Eternal life. It is known as the original cross, which is a powerful symbol that was first created by Africans in Ancient Egypt. The Ankh also resembles a key and is considered the key to eternal life after death. Its influence was felt in every dynastic period and survives as an icon possessing mystical power throughout the Coptic Christian era.

## Egyptian Initiation
### (Neo-History)

[I remember a great deal of details around past lives in Ancient Egypt. I was instrumental in the creation of the Mystery Schools. I also have recalled and have had channels tell me about my role in the entire setup of the Great Pyramids and topography of the entire layout around the structures and Hall of Records. I remember sealing the Hall of Records and placing the 7th Seal Sigil on the door. I am adding this now in my revision to share what I was unwilling to share in the past. I was instructed by Spirit that I was not allowed to come out with everything I had been shown or the things I knew in my own access until the time was right.]

It was nearly a life long task to undergo the quest of a neophyte. The individual had to graduate from the two schools of the two eyes of Horus, of which, each lasted 11 years. When they reach 33 years of age they where permitted to receive the Greater Mysteries, from the inner Chamber of Light. This was where Akhenaton, rather his Grand Hierophant completed the initiation by providing the actual remaining process of true ascension.

There was a great deal of information that was added at the time of Akhenaton, filling out what had been missing, or lost over thousand of years, from the two schools, regarding the entire teachings of the right and left eyes of Horus.

The whole body of teaching respectively represented the Right and Left brain teachings of Body and Mind or Emotions and Intellect. The ceremony of the ascension would take place on a very auspicious date when there were significant energetic alignments in the planetary and celestial bodies. This was desired because of the refraction and amplification of the subtle energies that would be channeled or focused into the sarcophagus in the King's chamber of the Great Pyramid. This would essentially jump-start the neophytes Merkaba and the corresponding fields of energy that extrudes, expanding and in intensifying, assisting in the process of initiation/activation.

Some very significant symbols, which represented actual tools for ascension where used to assist in preparing the initiated for the ceremony. The three main tools, which were the devices, that literally prepared the body through energetic attunement are; the staff of life, the hook and the flail. (More detail and understanding regarding these instruments and methods will be covered in part two of this book.) The procedure was accomplished by placing the staff of life or tuning rod device to the base of the skull and running the hook shaped device up and down the length of the rod. All while the flange or three parts of the flail was held in the air over the initiates' head to channel higher more focused energies into the body. This whole process was primarily designed to activate the kundalini, open and attune all the chakras to ensure that the body/mind system was clear and on-line, so to speak, ensuring that the individual was as open, aligned and activated as possible to ensure the success of the Merkaba ignition.

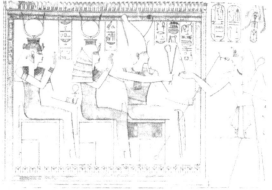

*Receiving the right to undergo the finale initiation*

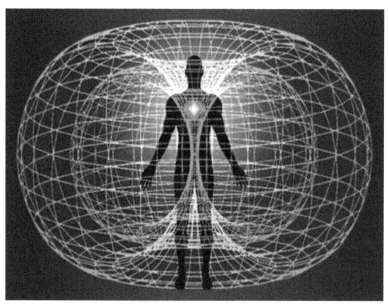
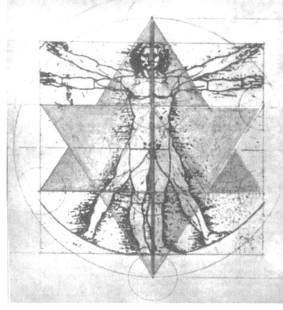

# Kings Resurrected
### (Gnosis / Neo-History)

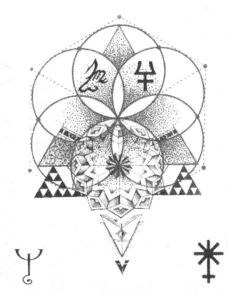

*The Writers of the script and the Actors of the play are side by side with the Directors and Produces on center stage experiencing the finale act together as one grand performance.* [We are all duplicates of the original 12 of the 24. This was what I remembered when I was 26 years old and when I was 29 I meet the woman who was aware she was the oversoul fully embodied here as the 'head quarter', so to speak, of all her selves in all of existence. I introduced her to Cosmo. That was some really incredible stories! We all confirmed what we knew, which is that we are the Eternals who are aware of our multidimensional selves. She said we have pyramid installations on many planets and have versions of ourselves in suspended animation under the pyramids or in them. Drunvalo Melchizedek said some very similar, as did Larry Hunter, which the head guard of the Great Pyramid told him. There was a sleeping man in a secret chamber in the Great Pyramid, which was removed.]

The kind of preparation that must go into the unfolding of the divine plan is most amazing and intricate. We may often notice the interesting connections between souls and their soul groups, which they incarnate with. For example, the mother of Jesus was a part of the immediate family or circle of close friends during the ascension mystery school there in Egypt. It is interesting to note that Drunvalo Melchizedek's says that Mary retreated into the great city, which lies some 500 meters below the surface, where she awaited the next great time of service with Jesus.

These type of major events that have been staged to assist humanity in its hour of awakening merit much more attention and research than has currently been provided. It is clear that we are nearing another paramount emergence of the white brotherhoods front line maneuvers. It has come to my attention that the awareness of the forces that have been the main ground crew, so to speak, will behoove the inhabitants of the planet in their greater realization. The full disclosure that will be presented through out this entire work, regarding the cadre of saints that have assisted time and time again, will serve in readiness for their imminent return.

On this note briefly, I would like to mention that in Dr Josua David Stones Ascension Manual it states that his communications with the Masters revealed this:

*"If what I have mentioned so far isn't amazing enough, also on this planet now are forty senior members of the Spiritual Hierarchy who have come from Spiritual planes and have externalized physical bodies as the Lord Maitreya to help and support him in his work. Ten of these Masters, Djwhal Khul has told us, have actually materialized physical bodies as the Lord Maitreya has. Another ten or fifteen are overshadowing their disciples and initiates as the Lord Maitreya did with Jesus. The other ten or fifteen have incarnated into babies' bodies and are growing up or have grown into adulthood already"*

*"One of these Masters is referred to as John of Penial, although that is not his real name. He is the incarnation of John the Beloved, the disciple of Jesus who ascended in that life who ascended in that lifetime. He is an incarnation of the Master Kuthumi. Djwhal has told me that Masters at that level can incarnate in more than one personality at the same time. He is the great Master that Paul Solomon, the modern-day Edgar Cayce, who will open the Hall of Records in the Great Pyramid and Sphinx and release all the Atlantean Records. Djwhal has also said that St. Germain, Hilarion, and Paul the Venetian are involved with the process of externalization."*

We shall see great relevance to these words portrayed here in this work, as well as many synchronicities regarding the players and their roles.

Another interesting synchronicity; which was of divine timing or an intervention at best, was when the Father of Amenhotep III; Tutmoses IV was told by a voice while passing by the sphinx, which was covered to the neck in sand at the time. "If you remove the sand from around me I will make you a great Pharaoh, and your children will do great things for the return of Egypt to her heights of glory". So he did as instructed and of course he became Pharaoh and his son was one of the greatest minds of all time, implementing structures that where nearly the equal in geometry and aesthetics of the old times. This young man found an entrance to the underground complex, which will become the pivotal piece in the full story of what ensued in the coming years of his grandson's time (Akhenaton). The direct result of this discovery was the reinstating of the forefathers use of the Sphinx and its subterranean temples, chambers and rites. This was why Akhenaton ended up calling himself *the High Priest of Hor-em-akhty*; the Sphinx complex. The

Egyptian mystery school at the time of Akhenaton was the purest and most complete teaching since the original installment of 10,500 BC. Its demise was as great a travesty, even greater than the burning of the Alexandrian Library. **[However, Cosmo told me that all the important manuscripts were copied and saved in another location.]**

This new mystery school was built or setup upon the existent mystery school of Amenhotep III, which was fairly close to a full understanding of complete wisdom. It had a great deal of the intellectual understanding and some of the emotional/intuitive knowledge, however it was lacking in the metaphysical and quantum physics related material that enable the full expression of a technologically advanced civilization ranging in harmony through spiritual to technological. This was to be accomplished by the reestablishment of the secret order of the renewed eternal priesthood by Tutmoses IV. It has also been known that there was a form of a cult that had been worshiping the Aten (Akhenaton's sun with hands, representing the One Creator,; Aten is the symbol and name for the consciousness behind the sun or Divine consciousness.) in secret several years before his time. Great insight into this time and the mysteries surrounding Akhenaton will be revealed in part two.

The military and old government faction assassinated Akhenaton after seventeen years of his reign. His stepbrothers' only son Tutankhamen and Akhenaton's daughter was succeeded to the throne at the age of 7. King Tut was very adept in his father's teachings and was a very self-aware young man. (The identity of his true father will remain a mystery until nearly the end of the book, as we to build and prepare a newly balanced consciousness for the full implications of the release this new information. As well as, the significance of Nefertiti in this entire story.) He and his twin flame would attempt to reinstate the fully active Mystery School of Ascension and prepare for the next golden age together as One Divine reflection back on the throne of the old empire.

Although the Dark Priesthood kept a close watch on them and when it became evident what they where attempting to do in secret, King Tut was also assassinated at the age of 19. Sadly, much of the precious truths revealed then, were lost to the sands of time.

Probably the single most paramount piece of secret knowledge that remains is the need for balance between the two aspects of self, the male and female polarities. The greater this balance was in harmony the more self-aware the individual became. This truth can be seen throughout Egypt in so many ways. The symbol of the two eyes of Horus shown at the same time represented the state of Self-Realization or Enlightenment. In association with the meaning of the two eyes, the symbol of the Ankh was the very ancient sign for life and ascension; it represented the balance of the polarities and the unity of wholeness. The top half of the glyph was representative of the female or vagina and uterus and the bottom half represented the male or penis inserted into the vagina as a symbol of unity or oneness.

This is a most exciting story that is probably the greatest enigma of our time, with much speculation regarding what actually happened. The surviving evidence is rather limited, and what there is presents many twists and turns in the potential story line. This is the story that is most compelling to me because it is the one that Spirit has guided and prompted me to discover and remember my entire life in many profound ways, some of which will be shared in entirety as we proceed.

There will be many revealing insights to offer regarding the entire story as I have come to recall it, as well as through piecing together the obscure fragments. Much of this came in a flash of completion or fruition on my second trip to Egypt. As we continue to sweep away the layers of dust and sand, the whole story will become more and more obvious.

*Resurrected Osiris*

## Ascension Tools
*(Gnosis)*

*There are several symbols that represent key aspects to the underlying wisdom being revealed.* ✶

There are so many symbols and images that are used to tell the bigger picture or complete story in ancient Egypt. We will be looking at the ones that are central to the understanding of

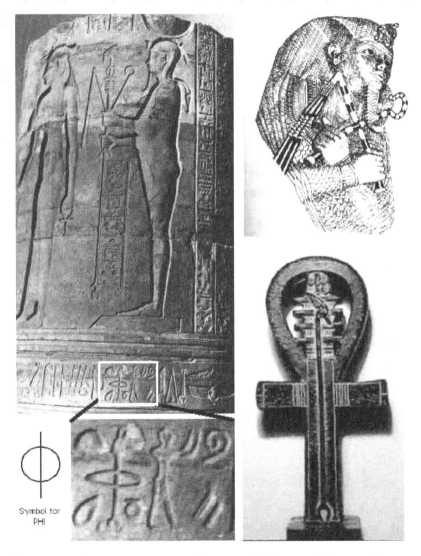

Symbol for PHI

the ascending consciousness or accessing our higher wisdom and expanded awareness potential.

The Ascension Tools where so significant in the rites and ceremony of Ascension that the symbols where superimposed on the Ankh; this one here representing Eternal Life through Ascension. With the symbol called the Djed as the central structure, which represented the spinal column of Osiris, as well as a divine child seated at the top of the spine indicating an awakened state. The hieroglyphics in the ceremonial picture to the left actually show the perfectly balanced state or the frequency of Phi, which is unconditional love. Additionally, notice the further significance emphasized by the figure that is worshiping in front of the symbol that resembles the golden spiral. These symbols were even buried with the dead because of the major role they played in Ascension; as seen in the picture above of King Tut.

**[I have assembled so many variables that are completely confirming the entire vision of a massive message preserved in stone and pictures. I am going to drop some bread crumbs in this chapter that shine light on the core ingredients. Lets see if this speaks to the inner wisdom of your soul. The next pictures and information until the end of this chapter is all a new revision to this original material. This will be shown with the aid of a lot of pictures. I created over 3,000 slides for power points over the last decade to emphasis the details.]**

Was there a WAY? A means to go to the afterlife. The following images tell the story of the belief in a visual manner.

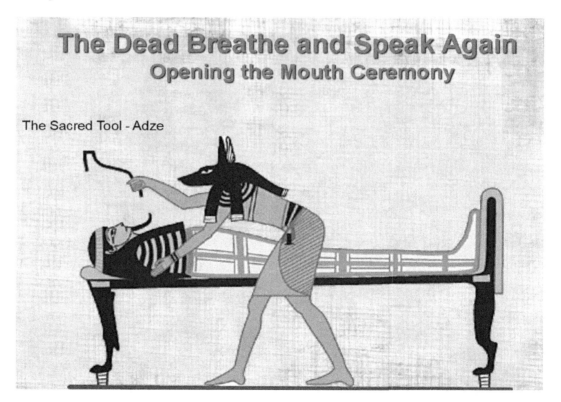

Many Bulls were sacrificed and buried with the King. Why was this really done? It is said that the Apis was very sacred. Is there more to this? Why was the leg of the bull cut off in these images? Did it have something to do with showing the WAY to Ascension or to the Golden Gate, where the soul can ascend into a higher dimension? We will learn the answer to these questions and so much more as we proceed.

Is there any answers in the tools? Let's look deeper, as we created the foundational understanding.

The symbol that represents the tool that opens the mouth, allowing the body to speak into other dimensions is the leg of the bull. What does it also resemble? There are also a variety of other tools involved in this process too. All these bits and pieces will be pulled together to deliver a meaningful and fuller picture as we proceed.

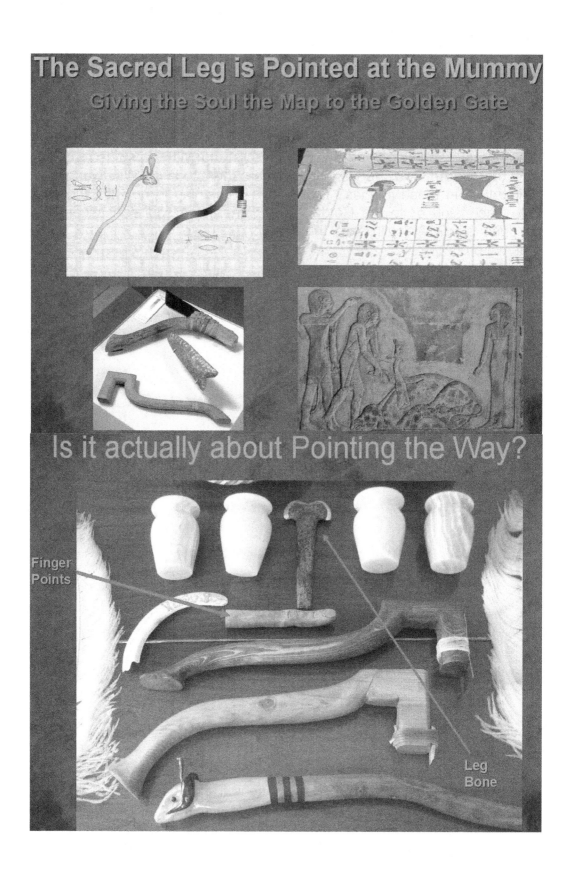

There is a very well explained message that all these images portray. My inner knowing knew there was a hidden core value that explained that we came from the stars and that we return to the stars, or the higher dimensions. It really is rather miraculous that a message of this magnitude was preserved in so many ways! I will take some assembling of a variety of parts to convey the full picture. The map and the message is what is underlying in all that I was innately intuiting.

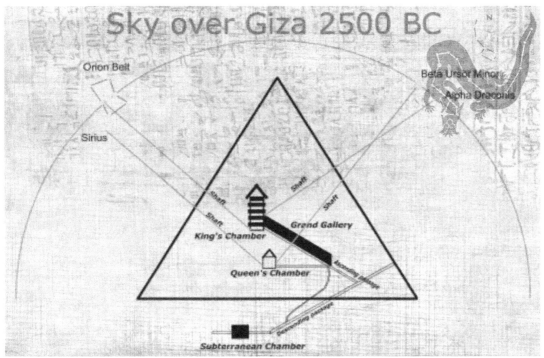

What was so important about these locations that shafts of perfect precision pointed to these locations in the sky?

**The Dragon and the Bear are at the center or the axis of the story.**

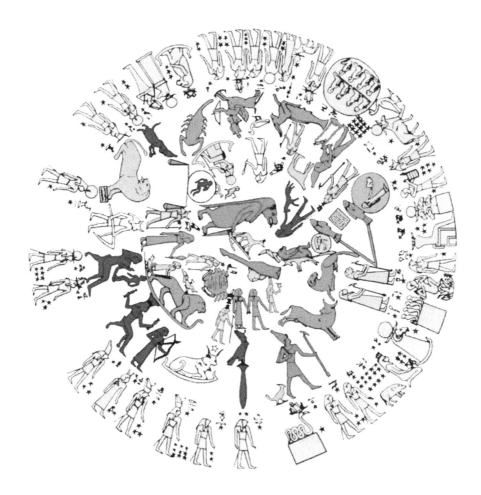

The ceiling of Dendarah - Temple of Hathor (Look at the Center) The complete Zodiac and the 36 Decans are depicted. Isnt amazing that all ancient cultures had the same images telling the same story? Is there a Gospel in the Stars?

Did you see the Leg?

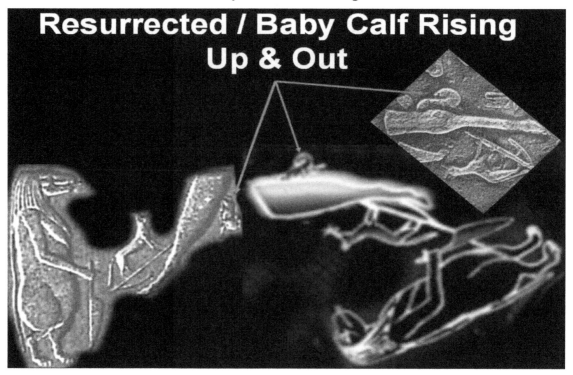

And the little re-born calf? Also pictured is the Hippo with the Knife. The Hippo is the Mother of the Nile, the Nile is the Milky Way.

### Along the Path

- **Anubis** - Gate Keeper
- **Protector** of the Dead and the Gate to the Afterlife
- **Central figure** in the middle of the Egyptian Zodiac

There are a great many things that could be further stated about all these characters, suffix it to say, there is a central theme that I am highlighting to deliver the throughput of this greater interpretation. One that has been exuding from my higher self my entire life.

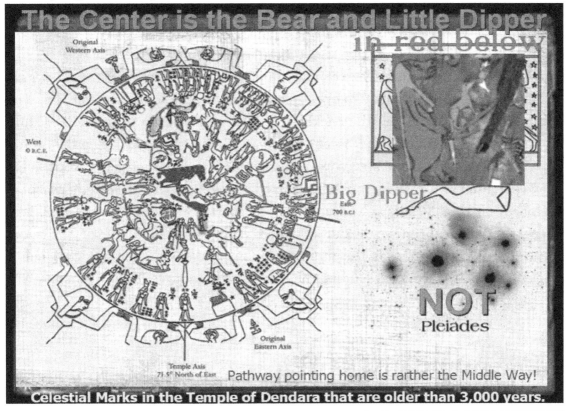
Celestial Marks in the Temple of Dendara that are older than 3,000 years.

Divine Alignment - Golden Age Activation - Mirrors the Topography of Giza

# Osiris's Backbone
(Neo-History)

*Here is another symbol that is part of the stage, each prop will fit into the greater scene and complete the full wisdom disclosure.*

The Djed is one of the most powerful symbols in all of Egypt, it encompasses the enlightenment factor of the two open eyes, as well as the tools of ascension. This symbol literally represents the backbone of Osiris, for when fully realized, fully on-line with the divine; the ascended being is the vanguard or pillar of the spiritually balanced social structure. This symbol represents the active principal of divine intervention via the sable Melchizedek Priesthood with it ascended members both materialized and unseen. The majority of these pieces that have been found have been made out of wood. This is because one of the secret meanings of this symbol is the tree of wisdom. Is this technology or a ladder representing the stages of ascending the cosmos to the source of consciousness?

*Djed*

# Serapis the Gnostic Egyptian
*(Gnosis/Neo-History)*

*Introducing another key player who is paramount in the overall story that is playing out here within these pages and throughout the Neo-History or in a great way, revealing a HER-STORY!*

There were several prominent figures or characters in the esoteric vein of the Gods of Wisdom. Are all these various characters part of a bigger wheel of characters that tell a fuller story about who we are and where we come from, or even perhaps to we return? There are key central figures that are important to understand in assembling the wider view point that reveals a world wide ancient wisdom.

We will look at a couple of the prominent ones that are integral to the work being presented here. One of the most noteworthy is Serapis, who plays a major role in the Neo-History story that will be unfolded throughout this material. He is also known by the appellation: Serapis Bey, who is an Ascend Master whose ether temple sits over Luxor. . 

The Greeks and the Gnostics both revered Serapis Bey with the highest of veneration. He had a special temple and mystery school in Alexandria, Egypt, where he was honored as a Creator Being. He was known as the Keeper of the Greater Mysteries and as the Sacred "Androgynous" Snake. These ancient cultures understood the secret meaning of the Snake, which actually was known for being the wisest, as well as representing the creational life force, kundalini and the deeper understanding of the DNA. There are a variety of ways the snake shows up in all these creation myths, as well as the one where Sophia takes the form of a snake in the apple tree to inform Eve of the ill intent of the Chief Ruler, in addition to a wealth of other information from Egypt about the positive aspects of the snake.

We will look further at these as we proceed as they are also central to the greater understanding.

Serapis's Temple when ransacked in AD 85, by the edict of Theodosius, the greatest exterminator of the pagan cult religion, yielded a wealth of symbols and information concerning the rituals of the higher degrees of the Egyptian Mysteries. It was reported that the statue of Serapis was thirteen feet tall and made of what look like emerald. When the Christians tried to destroy it, they struck the statue with an ax and the instrument was instantly shattered into dozen of fragments, with sparks flying all about.

At that time, several figures of Serapis stood in various temples in Egypt and Rome; gradually Serapis usurped the positions previously occupied by the other Egyptian and Greek gods and became the supreme deity of both religions. The Hebrew, Serapis is Saraph, meaning, "To blaze up", for this reason the Jews designated one of their hierarchies of spiritual beings the name Seraphim (literally; fire serpents). Serapis's strong influence continued until well into the fourth century, when his demise was cause by the famous edict: "De Idolo Serapidis Diruendo", denouncing Serapis as Idol worship. There are several very interesting accounts of Serapis's temple and its connection to the Gnostics preserved in old manuscripts. It is most beneficial to recount the following here, to further support what is being portrayed in this work.

> *"The Gnostic Mystics were acquainted with the arcane meaning of Serapis, and through the medium of Gnosticism this God became inextricably associated with the early Christians. (Gnostics) In fact, the Emperor Hadrian, while traveling in Egypt (AD 134), learned that the worshippers of Serapis where Christian and that the Bishops of the Church also worshiped at Serapis's Temple. Hadrian even declared that even the Patriarch himself, when in Egypt adored Serapis as a Christ."* (The Patriach would have been equvillant to the Pope.)

Some very profound information about Serapis has survived down through the ages, as well as some very good channeled information revealing and supporting his connections throughout time. Mark Prophet channeled some pertinent information concerning his connections in Egypt; Serapis has an etheric temple over Luxor, which is where the wisdom or flame of ascension is kept, thus he is called and known as the Keeper of the Ascension Flame. According to Prophet

Serapis was the incarnation of Amenhotep III, who had the complex and temple at Luxor built, which is a geometrical and mathematical wonder. All of the knowledge and wisdom of such understandings is displayed in the architecture there.

We will come to see that Prophet's channeled information was close to the full truth, though not exact, in regards to who Serapis actually was at the time of Amenhotep III's the surrogate father of Akhenaton. This will be evidenced by several profound confirmations.

The Greeks honored Serapis as the God of Philosophy and Science, even though his origin was in Egypt as Asar-Hapi. Serapis was certainly well known in Egypt, though there was a more esoteric story, which was hidden behind the veil of mysteries, as he was a Keeper of the Mysteries himself. Prophet, further states that Serapis was one of the very early kings of Egypt, in addition, to being a High Priest of Ascension in Atlantis.

*Serapis*

# Pythagoras
(Neo-History)

*Many of the players in the play will be seen wearing the same costume.* ✳

The Greek Pythagoras was born around 600 BC. His Father Mnesarcus and Mother Parthenis were in the city of Delphi doing merchant business, when they decided to consult the oracle as to whether the fates of the gods were favorable for their return voyage home. When the prophetess seated herself on the golden tripod, her response was not the question asked, she instead told them that Parthenis was with child and would give birth to a son who was destined to surpass all men in beauty and wisdom, and throughout the course of his life would contribute to the benefit of humankind.

Mnesarcus was so impressed he changed his wife's name to Pythasis, in honor of the Pythian priestess. When the child was born a son, they named him Pythagoras because the oracle predestined him. This story has many striking similarities to the birth of Jesus. They both were born when their parents were on a journey, both parents informed of the birth of a great son to be benefactors to humankind. In addition, both fathers were told by angels or holy Spirits that they were not to have contact with their wives during the pregnancies.

Pythagoras was also known as the "son of God", and was believed by the multitudes to be under divine inspiration. He traveled to many mystery schools to learn the secret ways; he was initiated in the great wisdom of the Egyptians, Babylonians and the Chaldeans. Pythagoras was the first to coin the term Philosopher for which he defined as "*one who is attempting to find out*". Before that time the wise men where called Sages, for *those who know*. After much wandering, he started a mystery school in Cortona,, Greece, where he gathered around him a small group of sincere disciples whom he instructed in the secret wisdom, which had been revealed to him.

He later married one of his disciples and had seven children. He lived to be 100 years old before he was murdered along with several of his disciples. The individual who committed this tragedy came to believe that Pythagoras teachings were false propaganda.. A man whom Pythagoras refused to admit into his circle of disciples instigated the suspicion. The surviving disciples attempted to perpetuate his doctrines, but were persecuted. Unfortunately, little remains today concerning the testimonials to the greatness of this Philosopher and his profound wisdom.

It is most, interesting to note that Aristotle records his thoughts on what Pythagoras taught as the following (This is extremely relevant to what we will learn and witness in the second part of this book):

> *At the same time, and even earlier, the so-called Pythagoreans attached themselves to the mathematics and were the first to advance that science by their education, in which they were led to suppose that the principles of mathematics are the principles of all things. So as numbers are logically first among principles, and as they fancied they could perceive in numbers many analogues of what is and what comes into being, much more readily than fire and earth and water (such and such a property of number being justice, and such and such another soul or mind, and so on with all the individual cases), and since they further observed that the properties and determining ratios of harmonies depended on numbers, since, in fact, everything else manifestly appeared to be modeled in its entire character on numbers, and numbers to be the ultimate things in the whole universe, they became convinced that the elements of numbers are the elements of everything, and that the whole "Heaven" is harmony and number."*

What is also known today is that Pythagoras understandings of creation and the human were very closely related to that of the beliefs of the Gnostics. For example; that we are really divine spirits experiencing this mortal coil of reincarnation until we become wise enough to become one with the immortals. He taught that the natural laws were present in math, music, astronomy, art, science and anatomy. He was a vegetarian, and was very adept at homeopathic herbal remedies. He even had tones you could listen to for specific aliments that would speed your recovery.

In his school, they had various levels or degrees that you would advance to, as you were ready to attain the wisdom of that next higher level. This process of attaining the inner most sacred of sacred mysteries was only to be revealed when the initiate could prove that he was ready to know the unknown.

These mysteries were concealed in symbols, otherwise, the knowledge was never written down, but only passed orally. One of the most sacred of symbols of the sect was the pentagon with a pentagram inside of it. As we shall see, this geometric shape and its number would play a very significant role in all mystery schools for it truly is divine.

*Did the ancients in fact truly understand the secrets of the creation of the universe with its codes and formulas, namely the existence of a language of light, which is only attainable by realizing the symbolic value of numbers and shapes?*

*Pythagoras*

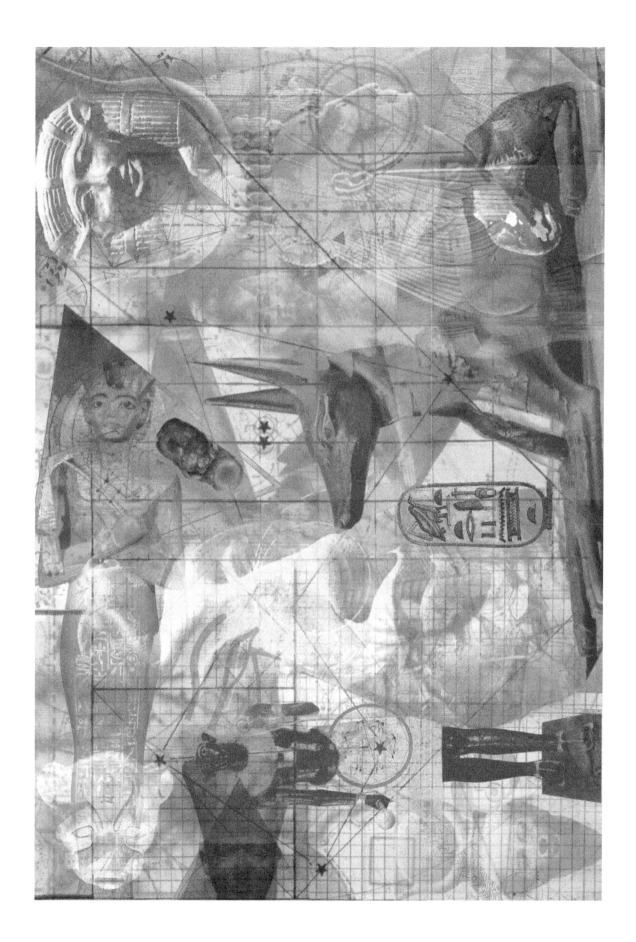

THE 7TH SEAL

# The Divine Ratio of Proportions
(Sacred Geometry)

*Following are several more primary ingredients necessary to understand the whole design.* ✳

Now let us return to the sacred science of the mystery schools. Here we will continue to build a foundation that we then can erect a great monolithic structure upon. From here forward, we will be doing a bit of weaving back and forth between the right-brain and the left-brain regarding the material that is being presented. This is designed to bring alignment and balance in a fuller understanding of how the mystery schools actually taught their initiates. The corner stone of Egypt was literally Phi; which inherently was known as many things; Golden Ratio, Sacred Cut, Golden Mean, Golden Section, and the Golden Rectangle. This is by far the most significant mathematical wonder that can be found replete throughout Egypt.

Phi carries the greatest significance and mystery behind it for all things ultimately come from it. In order to fully appreciate and understand what is being presented here in this book it is necessary to have a fairly sound grasp of the fundamentals of Phi. Over the next couple chapters Phi will be explained in general terms, simplify it's general function and value. We have already seen how the Fibonacci Series is intimately connected to the creation of all nature. Would it surprise you that the Fibonacci Series and Phi are also intimately connected? Perhaps not, since literally all things are interconnected. However, this relationship is so connected that in fact they are absolutely one in the same, only revealing themselves in different ways. So, it depends what you are looking at and how, as to what you will actually see. The symbol that is used to represent Phi is the 21st letter of the Greek alphabet, shown as a zero with a line through it. (ø)

We know that the ratio of Phi is 1.618, and we now know what that looks like in terms of a wave or flowing line on a graph. However, what does it look like expressed in form or architecture. Well, before we see that, we need to know what we are looking for. Therefore, let us start with a simple understanding of what the ratio or proportion of what Phi actually looks like. In the top portion of the diagram on the next page, the mathematical equation is expressed as a line divided at the ratio or proportion, which is Phi in relation to the over all line. The expression is stated as: the ratio of the longer part to the whole is equal to the ratio of the shorter part to the longer.

Moreover, what we see represented below in figure 2 is a Golden Mean Rectangle with the division at the appropriate place for the phi ratio. This is demonstrating an easy way to establish an exact phi ratio. It can be accomplished by drawing a square of any size. Then placing the compass needle on the half way mark on the top of the square and the other point on the left pr right bottom corner of the square, complete the circle. Then draw a horizontal line, which continues the top plane of the square out to meet the circle. This is the demarcation of the length of the phi rectangle or golden mean.

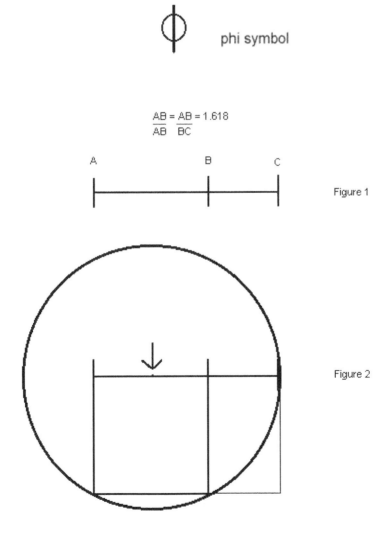

Figure 1

Figure 2

Additionally, one may use the numbers in relationship to the sequence of the Fibonacci to count out, as it were, the proportional relationship. For example, the follow diagram below demonstrates this, as well as the math.

Approximation of a golden rectangle (5 ÷ 8).

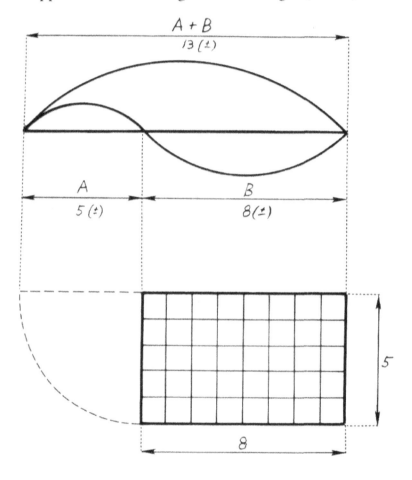

$A : B = B : (A+B) = 0.618...$    $B : A = (A+B) : B = 1.618...$

$5 : 8 = 0.625;\ 8 : 13 = 0.615$    $8 : 5 = 1.6;\ 13 : 8 = 1.62$

# The Sacred Cut
(Sacred-Geometry)

*This is one of the most important elements to understand that is a key to the universe. In several places this phrase as key will be seen and used to describe the way the meta-mechanics of the universe works. It is the back bone of several of the most important aspects of the code or glue that holds all of creation together!*

Now we can expand our understanding and see how the Fibonacci sequence is so intricately connected to the Golden Mean Rectangle that it could be called one and the same. Notice as we begin counting off squares, you begin to see the Golden Mean or Phi Ratio repeated over and over again.

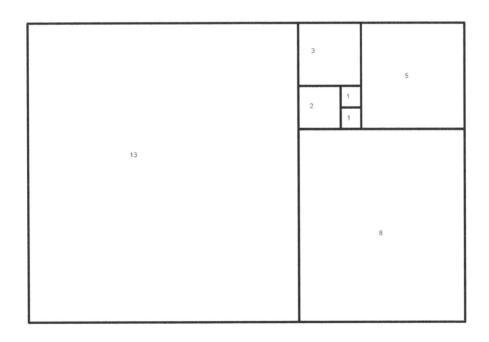

THE 7TH SEAL

As you can see, the Fibonacci sequence is perfectly intertwined or nested into the Golden Mean Rectangle. This is due to the Phi Ratio pattern of 1.618, which spaces the numbers out at that distance or ratio. This is also, where it begins to take on the value of recursion; where each term (i.e length duration) is determined by a formula according to the preceding term. The Egyptians where well aware of this and other natural laws that had been passed down to them, for they knew the importance of harmony and balance, seeking to express it in everything they did. The mystery schools preserved this knowledge about integrating thought and intelligence, with the balancing and harmonizing qualities of emotions to produce a natural science, as we shall see. The fundamentals and the foundation of their culture was setup to harmoniously blend science and spiritual. The use of Phi was very prominent in their art, as well as architecture. It provided balance and harmony to the structures and decorations that were not only pleasing to the eye aesthetically, but also structurally sound, as well as synergistic.

Therefore, below we see another example of the understanding of how the Golden Spiral is also directly connected to the Fibonacci sequence. Count the number of Squares for the length of the boxes and compare to the previous diagram on the last page.

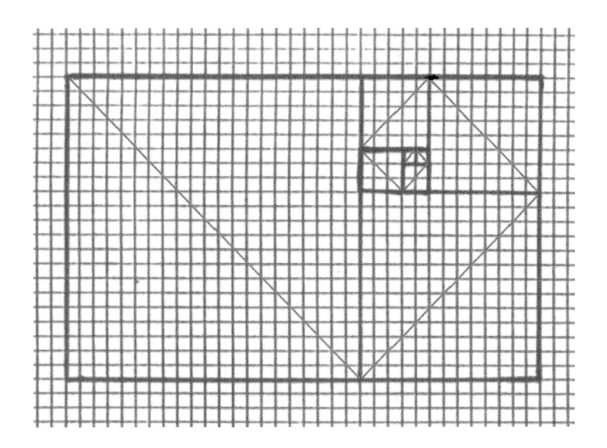

# Golden Spirals of Life
(Sacred Geometry)

This is where we begin to see the real possibilities of the interplay of all things as an integrated whole. Now let us move on with some additional aspects of Phi. Using this Phi/Fibonacci algorithm nature best optimizes space or placement, producing harmony and cadence in creation. The Phi ratio is literally a step-by-step problem solving procedure, especially in a computation of recursion, or the repetitiveness of patterns, such as holograms which are primarily of a recursive nature. We will return to the Golden Spiral a little later after we have established some more foundations for Gnosis.

Some of the math, which is required to understand these relationships, is not always easy for everyone to comprehend. So there are several different ways this is presented here to very easily see a visual representation of the interconnectedness of Phi, the Golden Mean Rectangle and the Great Pyramid, as well as other relations through the book.

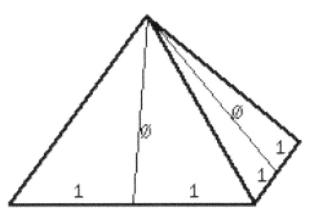

Above is how one representation of what a mathematical expression would look like for the relationship of Phi to the Great Pyramid. We will discover how this mathematical formula is expressed in easy to understand picture form. Essentially, each side of the pyramid is two 3, 4, 5 right triangles, back to back, which is another presentation of the dimensions of Phi.

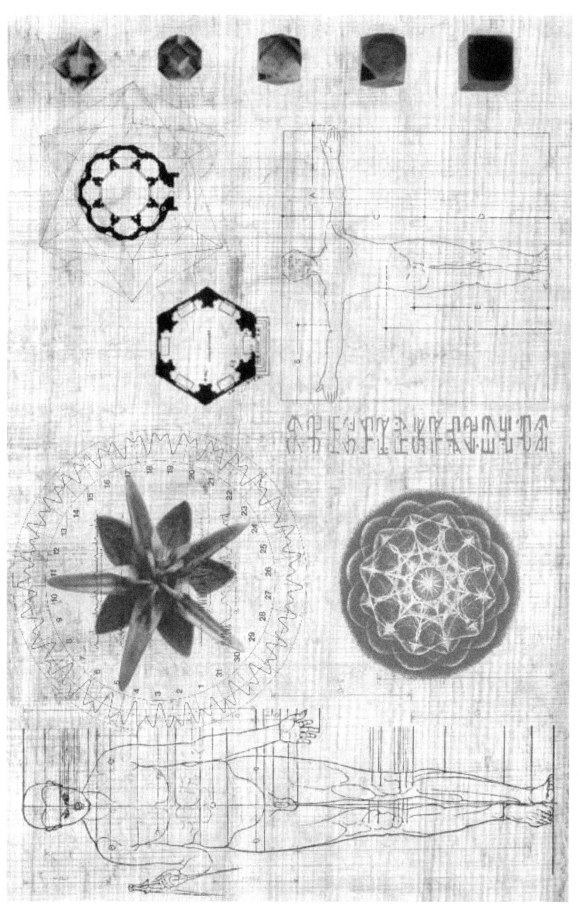

THE 7TH SEAL

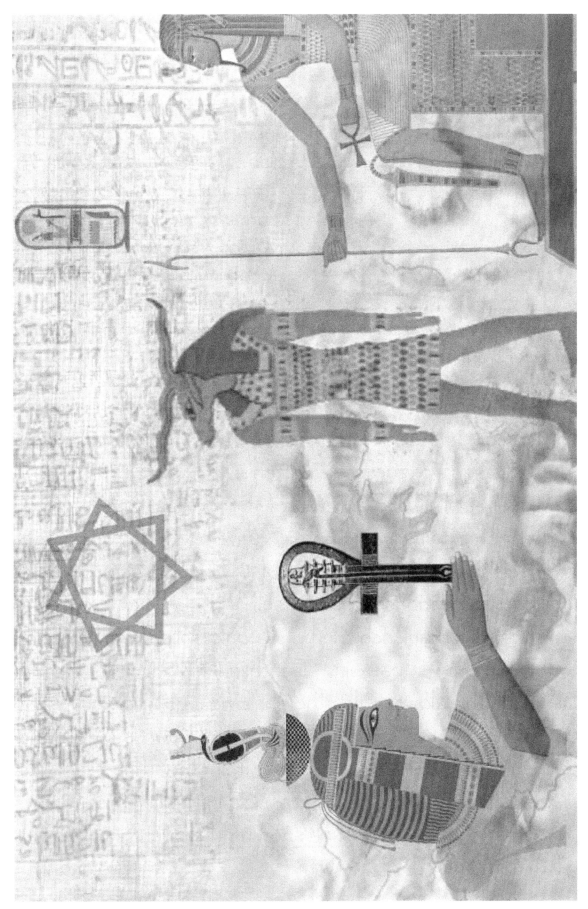

# Thoth's Flower of Life
(Sacred-Geometry)

*There will be several core keys, both in numbers and shapes. These keys are the real building blocks of Reality. The codes that correspond to the Sacred Geometry are integral to how the Divine Matrix functions. When the proper codes as number sequences are added to the images they activate the shape and its multidimensional energies. This is an over arching understanding that underpins all of this material and existence.*

The flower of life is a form of an enneagram, which is found in the Osirian Temple. It, along with a few other versions, is the only thing pictured or written in the temple. This is a universal symbol depicting all of creation; it has contained within it everything in creation. Drunvalo Melchizedek Flower of Life workshop details much of the sacred geometry and its interconnections to life itself. It is shown here to demonstrate that each of the platonic solids can be found within the flower pattern. Thoth, in his Emerald Tablets mentions the Flower (also the basic hexagon pattern) many times and its **_keys to eternal life_**. Also shown is Metatron's Cube (shown below), which is within the flower as well. These symbols were used extensively in the mystery schools for many reasons, as well as showing the interconnection of all things.

THE 7TH SEAL

## Metatron's Cube & Tree of Life

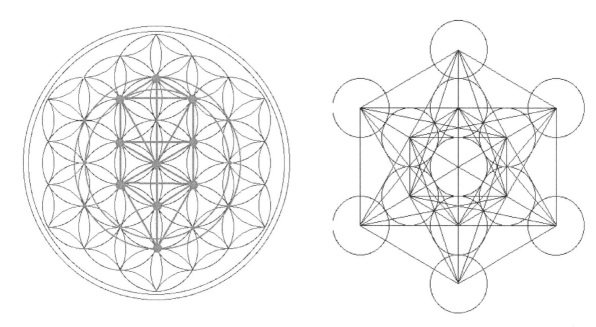

Flower of Life with the Tree of Life perfectly seated within the central 7 circles. 12 circles are around the outside of the flower. There are 19 circles in all. Visually and numerlogically they are all One (19 is 1 + 9 = 10 or 1).

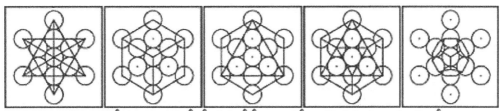

Five Platonic Solids Hidden within Metatron's Cube

# Phi Snake
(Gnosis)

*Many of the audience are awakening and realizing that they are more a part of the play than they first thought. Many are remembering various aspects of the entire design.* **[And Collectively we influence the outcome far more than we realized. I created this body of work to activate our higher consciousness so we could take more direct control of our lives and the world around us.]**

The Egyptians used many forms of symbolism; many of these images are still misunderstood till this day. The controversial snake is the subject matter of many religious discourses, although it is very evident that the Egyptians revered the snake as extremely sacred. Here we see several very explicit pictures, all of them being a representation of the same principle, i.e. Keys to Life. When you take the Golden Spiral and turn it, rendering it three dimensionally, it begins to change shape and starts to resemble a snake. While turning it you reach a point where you have the waveform, which we saw in the Fibonacci sequence graph earlier. This flowing line when fanned out like a deck of cards makes an image, which Dan Winter has called the Grail cup. You can see a wonderful animation of this at his site. (_____)

It clearly shows the recursive nature of this design, self-embedding into infinity; again completely supporting all information about the creative harmonizing nature of Phi. What we see pictured below is the Egyptian Snake of Eternal Life carrying the Ascended being home to the central sun. Another famous snake symbol is suggesting the eternal nature of the ever-changing expression of creation and all its infinite collective consciousness. **[We are going to learn many things about the snake, ancient beliefs and symbolism in this material. There is a considerable amount of dis-information about the meaning. There will be an entire chapter on this subject in the next volume.]**

Dan Winter's Grail Cup viewed from the side.

*Entrance into Knowledge of All Existing Things*
(Sacred Geometry)

The other very significant sacred geometrical underpinning of creation is the function and value of PI!

The simplest way of stating a terse understanding of Pi is as follows: "Pi is the number of times that a circle's diameter will fit around the circle."

Pi, like Phi, goes on forever, though Pi, unlike Phi, cannot be calculated to a perfect precision:

3.1415926535897932384626433832795028841971693993751....

Although, no apparent pattern emerges in the succession of digits ~ a predestined, yet unfathomable code it remains. The numbers do not even repeat periodically, yet seemingly popping up by blind chance; lacking any perceivable order, rule, reason, or design, they remain "random" integers, *ad infinitum*. This is very unusual, as we shall see, for order does in fact exist even in apparent chaos.

The earliest known reference to Pi occurs in a Middle Kingdom papyrus scroll, written around 1650 BC, by a scribe named Ahmes. He began scroll with the words: *"The Entrance into the Knowledge of All Existing Things"* and remarks in passing that he composed the scroll "in likeness to writings made of old." Towards the end of the scroll, which is composed of various mathematical problems and their solutions, the area of a circle is found using a rough sort of Pi.

Physicists have noted the ubiquity of Pi in nature. Pi is obvious in the disks of the moon and the sun. The double helix of DNA revolves around Pi. Pi hides in the rainbow, and sits in the pupil of the eye, and when a raindrop falls into water Pi emerges in the concentric spreading rings. Pi can be found in waves and ripples and spectra of all kinds, and therefore Pi occurs in colors and music.

A more detail explanation around Pi is as follows: *"Pi is the ratio between the circumference of a circle and its diameter (the straight line through its center)"*. That is to say, the circumference of any size circle is always 3.14159 times its diameter.

It is very significant to our study here to note that the entire geometric structure of the Great Pyramid is designed on the basis of Pi (3.14) and of course Phi (1.618). It would appear that these two functions are opposites of each other in several ways. First, with the most obvious comparison, Pi applies to the circumference (circle) and Phi applies to a distance (lines, rectangles, and triangles). These two are also at odds with one another by the production of decimals. Pi produces random chaos and Phi produces harmony and balance. The functions of these two constants share a common message: each representing unique parts of the whole, which is the message that reinforces our greater oneness.

It is also most interesting to note that the numerology of their respective values reflects the polarity or energy weave of numerology between the underlying male(positive) and female(negative) patterns of existence. Pi (3.14) equals 8, which is matter, and Phi (1.618) equals, 16 or 7 which is Spirit!

The Great Pyramid is a colossal message that balance is the key to everything. This will be shown in several ways throughout this book. The first and most obvious is the blending of Phi and Pi forming the perfect symmetric synergistic image that it is. Pi within the Great Pyramid is revealed by the angle of the slope (51 degrees 51 feet 14.3 inches) of the sides. This angle results in the Pyramid's vertical height bearing the same ratio to the perimeter of its base, which the radius of a circle bears to the circumference. In other words, the height of the Pyramid to its apex can be taken as the radius of a circle: the distance around the Pyramid is found to be exactly equal to the circumference of that circle. (See the example on the next page.)

# Geometric Construction of the Great Pyramid

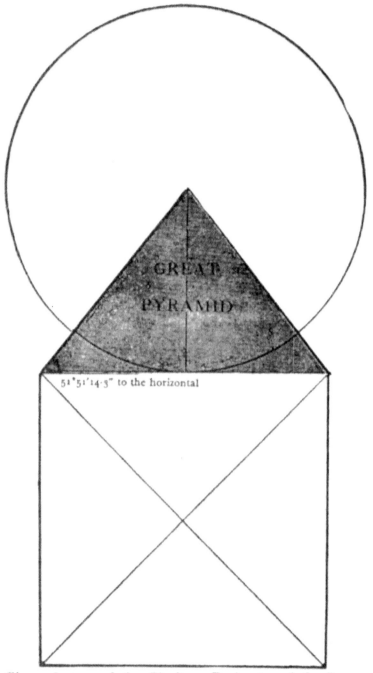

*Before the 1900's Pi and Phi were called transadental numbers, now science has named them the irrational numbers. The understanding of this shall become self-evident.*

# Seeing Phi between the Lines

(Sacred Geometry)

[I am encoding these pages with images, frequencies, codes and intention that activates a variety of things in you: memory, synchronicity increase and greater alignment to your higher self and guides. When you draw the 7th Seal image on the first page of this book, it activates into your field and has a very positive effect on your conscious evolution! Drawing Sacred G into your energy is a very good thing to do, such as learning to draw the flower of life as well. This definitely had a very valuable impact on my experience.]

Now we will look at a more left-brain approach to some of the symbolism, as we will always find a balance between the art and the science in the sacred symbolism. Can you see the phi ratio in this picture and can you identify the real phi-angel or 3-4-5 triangle?

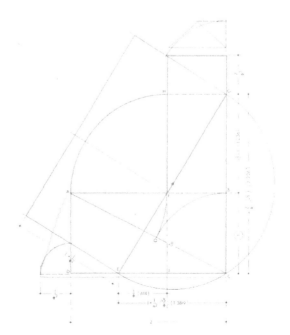

THE 7TH SEAL

This very sacred ceremony depicts the purification process for the opening of the mouth ritual, which is the procedure for giving the King his first breath of air into Eternal Life. There is a great deal of sacred geometry represented in this apparently simple figure.

Clearly there is a lot more going on here than meets the eye, let alone at first glance. There is more advanced math here that we need not indulge, a cursory understanding is all that is required to delve deeper into the greater mysteries that will arise out of the simple understanding of geometry and numerology.

More Phi and Pi in Egypt.

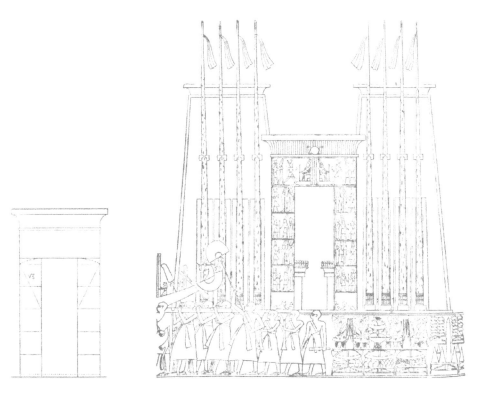

Above we see the sign for Pi built into this archway, which also contains the proportions of Phi. There is so much

deeper meaning is so many ways in all the imagery and design.

# Sacredness of Five
### (Neo-History / Gnosis)

*Numbers and symbols correspond in sacred cadence revealing layers of interconnecting hidden relevance.*

Why did the mystics revere the number 5 as such a sacred number? What is so special or unique about it? That it was raised above most all other numbers? One of the most obvious things that stand out is that we as human beings have five fingers and toes on each limb. As humans we also have 5 bodies; Physical, emotional, mental, astral, etheric. Well, there must be more to it than that and there certainly is, beyond that, we are divine and sacred. We will now see there are many unique qualities to the number 5.

It is also commonly known that the ancient Chinese's system of governing the body's health, uses a system of 5 elements; earth, wood, water, air, and metal.

In the Pythagoras numerology system the first number or vibration as unity was 1. From that absolute or whole, came a second entity which became two thus forming a duality. This entity was one half male and one half female. Sound familiar? This entity then split creating another entity that was the opposite. The male entity was numbered 2, and the other was numbered 3 and was female;

**2+3=5**. The opposites would attract as two magnetic poles and the energy that existed between these two was the emotion of love.

The Egyptians always drew their stars in the sky with 5 rays. Moreover, their quest in life was to return to the stars and become an immortal, eternal god. The human with outstretched arms and legs is also the formation of a 5-pointed star.

There are 5 faces to the pyramid, there are 5 courses or levels of block in the Kings chamber, there are 5 chambers above the Kings Chamber. The diameters of the shafts in both the King and Queen's chamber are 5 inches in diameter. Drunvalo Melchizedek teaches that there are 5 levels of consciousness with 5 sets of chromosomes corresponding to each. He also says there are 5 Melchizedek beings on the planet at this time. Many cultures say that we are going to become the 5th root race, i.e. The 5th generation of the complete Procession of the Equinox cycle.

The Mayans say that we are going to the 5th world and most metaphysical beliefs say we are on our way into the 5th dimension. My friend Cosmo tells of how we are preparing for the 5th generation *universe*, of which I will get more into later. In the Gnostic Scriptures, Jesus says if you are acquainted with the 5 trees in paradise, you will not taste death. The Gnostics also believed that 5 was the number of the Perfect Divine Human Being.

The word *Human* has 5 letters and the numerology on it yields 7, which is the number for Spirit. The Glyph for the number 5 is very unique in that it depicts Spirit joined to Matter, the circle represents Spirit, and the cube represents matter. 5 plus 7 equals 12, which takes us into another level of symbols, signs, and numerology.

Five unites Spirit with Matter to capture life and light into physical form, in essence 5 is embodiment. The Gnostics called Jesus the Great Epsilon. Perhaps the meaning and reason that he was giving this secret encoded name is now elucidated: the Greek word for the number 5 is Epsilon.

The pentagram is and was a sacred symbol of light, and health and vitality. Five was also understood esoterically as the number of Love, as well as the number of Life.

How many letters are there in the word LIGHT?

The five platonic solids are the basic building blocks of manifested form.

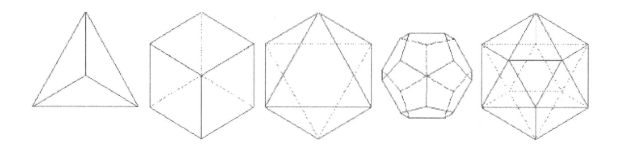

*Plato had his students hold and rotate these objects in their mind, while meditating on deeper levels of the interconnectedness of all things. This is only one aspect of several*

THE 7TH SEAL

*other paramount ingredients to finding the answers to the universe or discovering the greatest uncharted frontier in existence; inner space and self-realization.*

Let us now go another level deeper into the metaphysical and very important aspects of sacred geometry, where we will gain an understanding or Gnosis of the greater meaning of five, as Love & Life.

[The 5 Senses and the 5 vowels become a paramount part of the inner core values!]

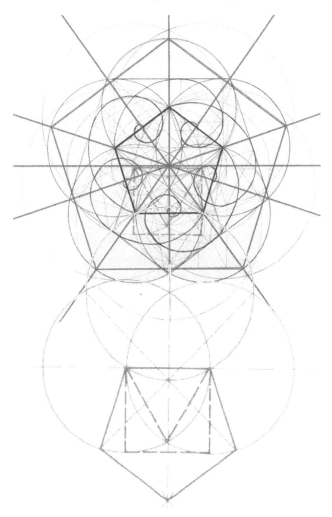

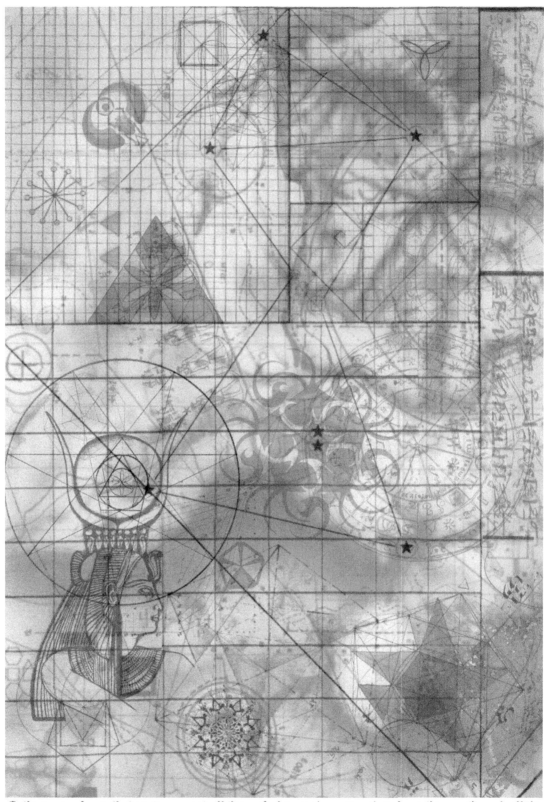

*Is there a road map that exists amongst all this underlying information that shows the way through all this ancient knowledge, ultimately leading to sacred wisdom? The answer is a resounding – YES! Stay tuned for each piece builds on the next revealing the whole picture in its grand completion.*

## The Esoteric Spirit of Five
(Sacred Geometry)

I believe by now you are really beginning to see how everything could be interconnected, and an integral part of the whole, even though the profoundness of the truth of unity and holistic oneness is so often overlooked by the world at large. We have the message of the ancients lovingly reminding us, when we stop to observe how the natural laws of the universe really work. It can be a very simple understanding, as I hope that I am demonstrating and desire to continue to elaborate more fully. With this next piece, we really begin to realize how everything is absolutely one and the same; light, sound, color and feelings are all just frequency and vibration, simply different ways of expressing the Light or energy of all that is.

For what we can come to understand is that Five and Phi are essentially one and the same as well. The number Five has the vibration of love because Phi is the frequency of love. The work that Dan Winters has done with a group of Medical Doctors clearly demonstrates the heartbeat at its most healthy rate, beats to the Phi ratio.

It was also found that at the moment of the feeling of unconditional love or compassion, you could see on the EKG monitor that the pattern formed was that of the waveform Phi ratio. This pattern and frequency are the templates of Life, for it is intelligence and consciousness as Light. This energy signature is what enables creation to pass on patterns of perfect symmetry, naturally forming creation and the regeneration of life.

Creation and manifestation is most easily accomplished with forms and shapes that have Phi within them, i.e. Pentagrams (shown on the next page).

Creation is a virtual matrix of endless nesting and embedding of geometric patterns occurring in a natural order; a perpetual self-organizing virtue. This is the sole basis for the fractals' reason to create irrational logic; this is how order emerges out of apparent chaos.

Another very good example of the intelligence inherent in the Phi ratio is demonstrated when you start to observe the shadows that are cast from shinning light at a Phi ratio spiral. What is revealed is that every letter in both the Hebrew and English language is created or shown in the formed shadow. Now that is really Self-Aware!

(Check out Stan Tenen's work at the Meru Foundation: www.meru.org)

Now we may begin to actually understand how the power of the spoken word is truly a language of light. Therefore, the vibration of love and life are really one and the same, a frequency that resonates as the Phi ratio.

So how does the number 5 fit in to this creation formula? One of its very unique qualities, which contribute to all of this harmony, is that when multiplied a multiple of 5, the result always has the number 5 in it, indicating the holographic nature of recursion. The only other number that does this is 6, which is another number that has some pretty profound esoteric meanings as well.

The number five has the numerological value of freedom and creativity. So in other words, freedom is an eternal or infinite number of choices for manifestations. When you put all this together, you have a formula for creation, which is self-loving, self-aware and self-existent. Phi is the self-evident natural language of the creators, created to encode the self-organizing unfolding of all of creation. It is found in galaxies, DNA, viruses, molecules, plants, minerals, and the anatomy of all creatures large and small. Phi and all of its qualities are what is innately required for communication and memory, i.e. Conscious existence.

How's that for a biological computer.

Now look at the photo below of a crop circle, do you see the simplicity of the message and the symbolism. Spirit encompasses and embraces all matter, everything is divine and when in Gnosis about the TRUTH of life, everything is just "PHI-ne" (FINE).

Crop circles are a sign of the times, with patterns of life in both symmetric and geometrical representation.

Some scientist that I have met (wishing to remain anonymous) reported that these crop circle locations actually have an unusual energy about them. They have conducted research that has revealed that what may actually be causing the phenomena is some type of plasma erupting from the earth. It was discovered that by viewing the areas through a particular type of lens from above, there could be seen geometric shapes and forms inside the plasma.

*The ancients understood these basic building blocks. And it is my theory that they understood so much more.*

**[That theory was proven out in a variety of ways, which are shown throughout my entire body of work. In fact, as I have been emphasizing more and more, I understood so much more than what I was willing to say back in 1998. I am now willing to come out with much more of what I am certain about. Especially**

regarding the Sacred Numbers and Meta-Numberology that I was laying the ground work for back then. In many ways I was way ahead of my time!]

# "Phi-ve" sided Magic
(Sacred Geometry)

[I recently found the Lost Gospel of Judas. This was very interesting and telling in a variety of ways. I will be adding this content to my videos and chapters here. It emphasizes the importance of five in a way that is very clearly directly tied to everything that is being explained here. Five senses and five vowels are indeed key, as we shall see!]

This is an exercise in discovering the hidden value inherent in the pentagon and the pentagram.

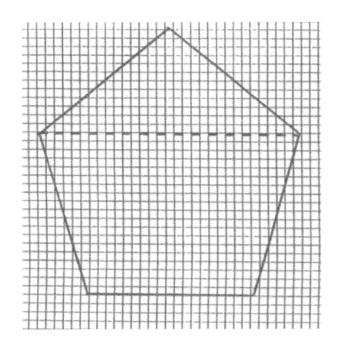

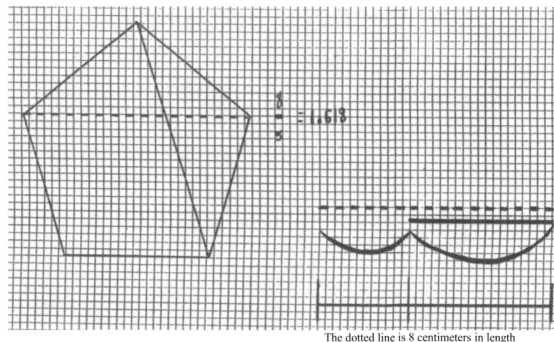

The dotted line is 8 centimeters in length
The solid line is 5 centimeters in length
**8 divided by 5 = 1.618 (Phi Ratio)**

Connect two sets of corners as depicted directly above and repeat all the way around. The length of the dotted line is 8 centimeters and the length of the full line is 5 centimeters; 5 divided by 8 / 1.618. The curve scale and bar key denotes the proportions.

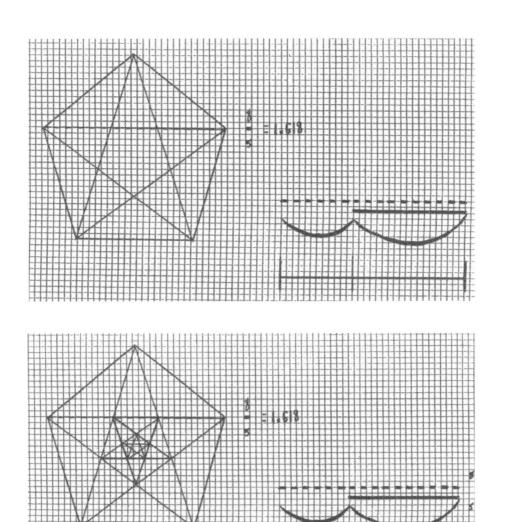

This reveals a great example of perfect symmetrical recursion in a series of interlocking pentagrams. The power of this symbol is nature in action. This symbol has been given a bad name, much like the swastika, which was an ancient power symbol of creation. Now we can certainly understand why Pythagoras chose to use this symbol as the signet of his Mystery School.

## Phi-ve Symmetry

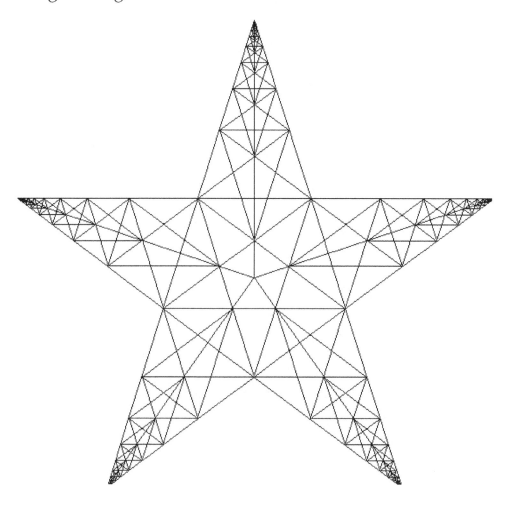

# The PHI of Life  (Sacred Geometry)

Below we see "Phi-ve" symmetry and a deeper look at the interconnectedness of all things.

Side View                Top View

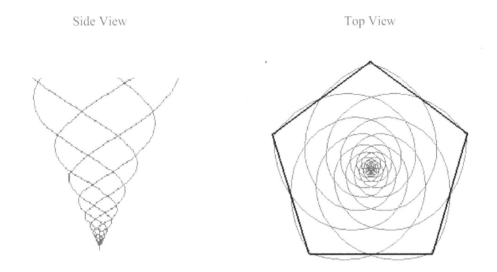

The Doceahedran below is 12 twelve nested Pentagons, rotating it left & spiraling it down creates DNA.

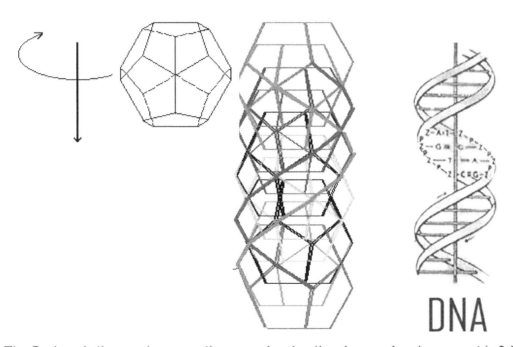

*The Dodeca is the most pro-creative, non-desctructive, harmoniously symmetric 3d model for natural nestting and embedding. It is the Mother of Fractal recurrsion, self-orginizing, self-aware algorithmic blueprint for life.*

# 3-4-5 PHI-Angle
*(Sacred Geometry)*

When Pythagoras was initiated in the mystery school in Phi – la – del – Phi – a, Egypt, where he learned all about the mysteries of Phi. One aspect of Phi, as we have seen in relation to certain triangles, are those with the ratio of Phi directly within them. The Egyptians loved to have secrets hidden within or behind the obvious, much like the other aspect of self that lies hidden within. The 3-4-5 triangle is just such a case; it is the Phi proportion which the Great Pyramid has hidden within it, so we find a "half of the Pyramid", breaking down into three parts, one built upon the other with the rule of Phi proportion. Here is a wonderful example of the sacredness of the 3-4-5 triangle encoding the mysteries of ascension in stone. Isn't it interesting that it is the depiction of a snake forming the 3-4-5 triangle.

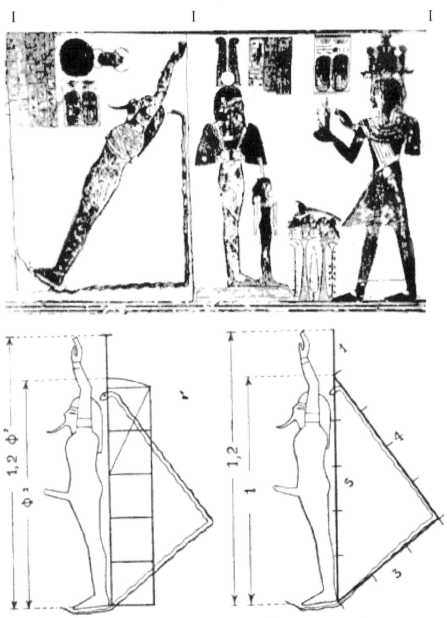

*This Glyph represents Ascension in the Great Pyramid.*

The Egyptians used the fuller understanding of the greater powers of Phi in many profound ways. Here are a few more ways of comprehending the proportional relationships of Phi.

This was done to aligning the subtle bodies of the initiate with the finer frequencies of the inter-dimensional spaces.

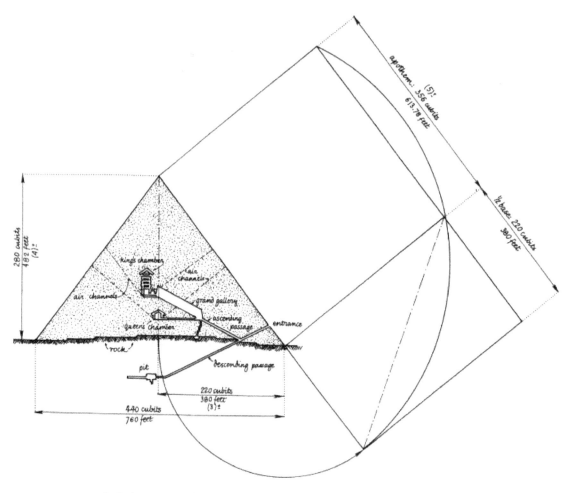

Great Pyramid of Cheops at Gizeh. Cross section shows that apothem and half the base are in golden section relationship.

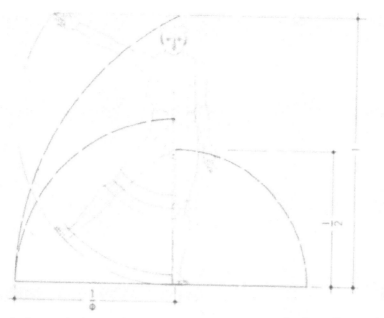

*The human body is in divine ratio proportion just as the Great Pyramid is.*

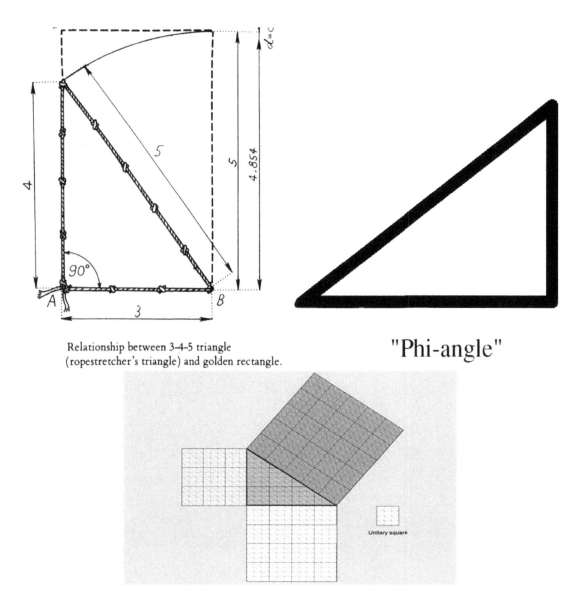

Relationship between 3-4-5 triangle (ropestretcher's triangle) and golden rectangle.

"Phi-angle"

It is most significant to note that the only true original writing or markings that exist inside the Great Pyramid is the "Phi-angle", which can only be seen in the appropriate lighting just above the exiting passage of the Kings Chamber. This is truly one picture that is worth a thousand words. Below is another example of the Divine proportions of the human being, further emphasizing the connection between the Great Pyramid and the perfectly manifested human form.

# Egyptian Proportions
## *(Sacred-Geometry)*

The Egyptians understood these secrets implicitly, for all the art, architecture and math that was used to build and decorate their temples was interconnected. They knew that this divine proportion was inherent in the living temple. If you look at your hand, you will see the Phi ratio starting with the tip of your finger through the first joint to the second as the dimensions or ratio of the golden rectangle. The same proportions exist from the top of your head to your navel, through to the bottom of your feet. Now notice from the tip of your fingers to the joint of your wrist on through to your elbow has the same proportion. This distance is Phi and the royal cubit as shown below.

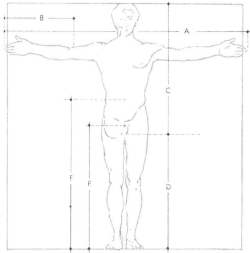

The 7th Seal

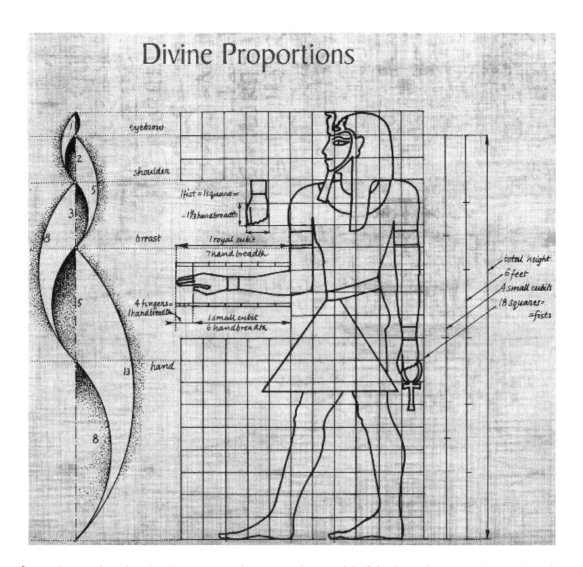

This is the template that the Egyptians used to create their model of the divine king on the temple walls, which reflects is also the exact method and unit of their measurement system.

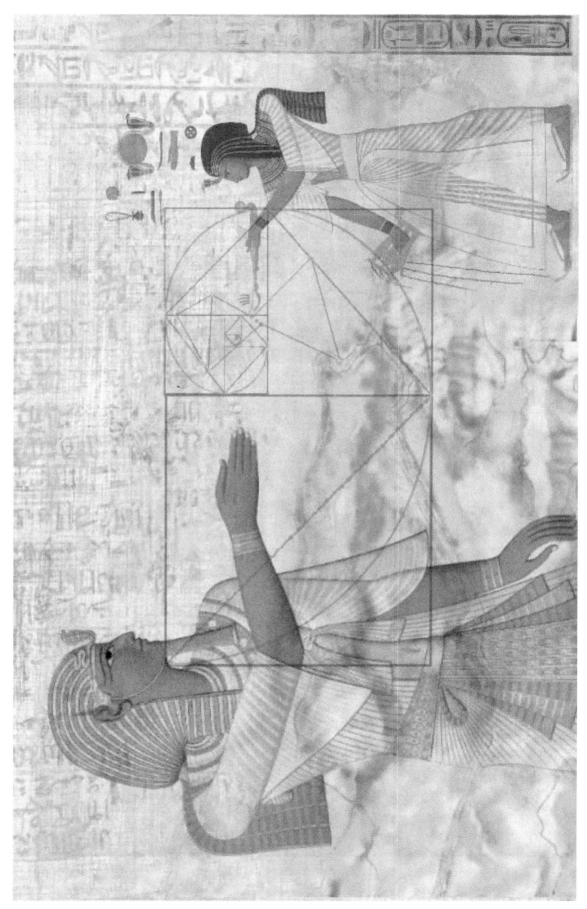

# Mystery in Egypt
*(Neo-History / Gnosis)*

Many Mysteries have been discovered in Egypt over the past decades, and many men and woman have attempted to solve them. It has been as if the Great Spirit of Egypt has not allowed her secrets to be fully known yet, until the appropriate time. In recent years, there have been several rather startling discoveries from secret chambers to lost knowledge. Many individuals have contributed to these discoveries and their understanding. One of the most profound to date is the Orion-Giza correlation, which is a message or map that has been preserved in alignment of the Pyramids, as well as within the greater layout of the structures on the ground within the Giza Plateau. This is the central theme of the work presented in this book. The discovery and understanding of this will reveal a most profound message of our true heritage.

The Giza Plateau has been situated in alignment with the star constellation of Orion as a focal point. This has begun to be recognized, remembered and awakened in humanities consciousness thanks to the work of Robert Bauva, author of the Orion Mystery and Larry Hunter. The work of Drunvalo Melchizedek have also revealed and made popular a great many things about Egypt and her lost ways. Many others have contributed to the unveiling and acceptance of the greater picture. We will learn more about those pieces as we continue to unfold this ancient scroll.

THE 7TH SEAL

What interested me the most was the layout of the Pyramids in relation to the Golden Spiral; it is here that I see many answers being silently given. For the spiral is literally a road map for the soul or ascending being to travel home; to the higher dimensions.

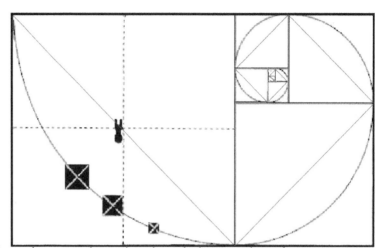

The message that I hear and see loud and clear is that the pattern or flight path, as it were, is nothing more than the vibration or frequency of unconditional love and compassion, i.e. the Phi ratio.

More than anything Love and compassion, are the single most important requirement or goal in the soul's evolution. This has been the message that has been taught from age to age. The message has been preserved in the world's greatest monument; the Great Pyramid. The wisdom contained therein is the key to all things; health, happiness, fulfillment and above all *Self-Love*. When we are in perfect resonance with this vibration all doors will open, inner and outer, as the hidden things of all times will be ours for the asking. This will be made crystal clear as we continue to galvanize our sacred temple; the human body.

I believe we are finally bringing balance and full awareness to our consciousness, awakening the divinity of our heritage, along with the totality of our harmonious body/mind systems. For the completed picture is the perfect blending of the polarities or properties of the male and the female, or in this case the scientific and the spiritual. Through this assimilation the greatest mystery of all will be revealed, the proof of life after death or Ascension; a conscious shift into higher realms or realities, the proof of the divinity of the Soul, and the proof of the unlimited potential of the human mind and spirit.

I believe the inner doors of all inner doors, the scientific wonder of the world will open her doors to the greatest kept secret of all times, the Hall of Records; the holy of holies. Through the alignment of the great cosmic clock and the reunification of the male and female archetype, the ancient lock or seal will be deactivated and the doors swung wide open for all the world to see, the truth about this planet, and the Divinity of You and Me. My life and path is this TRUTH!

# Gnostic Mystery
### (Neo-History / Gnosis)

The Gnostic Mystery School was one of the only schools to actually record much of the truths in written form about the Ascension and the knowledge of the true identity and eternality of the Soul and Spirit. Although some of its meanings were hidden or obscured, through metaphors and allegories the truth could and can still be found. One of the Gnostic sayings of Jesus was, *"I will complete you in the Mysteries of the Kingdom of Light"*, indicating that he would reveal or complete his followers with the Wisdom that had remained in the Mystery Schools. The fundamental premise of his mission was the fulfilling of the knowledge that we are Divine Spiritual beings in a material form. Jesus often used phrases like *"awakening us from our slumber"*, or expressing concern that he has come and *"found no one thirsty"*. He wanted to quench our thirst and remove the draught regarding the lost and forgotten truth about whom we truly are and what we are doing here.

The message was twofold; one aspect was reminding us or actually showing us how to re-establish *"acquaintance"* with our true selves (as the Children of Light, or the Perfect Divine Hu-man Race). The other produced the understanding that we are actually expressions of two different faculties, one Male or Mind and the other Female or Feelings. (Notice the M's and the F's.) The importance of the blending or marrying of the two aspects together in one harmonious balance of unity was the precise *way* to becoming the *Truth*. This message was almost completely lost or removed from the New Testament.

There are similar passages from another source within the same time frame, where we also find remnants of this truth preserved for example, in the Essene's Dead Sea Scrolls. The fundamental aspect of this unity message is clearly the most paramount requirement of Ascension into Mastery, or the reunification of the soul into the oversoul. We can see the key to this by looking at the Gnostic scripture which states:

*"The Parent of Eternity joined the virgin, and on that day he revealed the great Bridal Chamber and it was for this purpose that his (Jesus') body came into being (as the example and way). Just so that through these things Jesus made the entirety stand at rest with it; and it is befitting for each of the disciples to proceed into his (or her) repose." ~ Gospel of Thomas*

What we see emphasized is that the Bridal Chamber, which is the ceremony or initiation of the marriage of the two aspects of self in perfect unity or complete awareness of harmony in eternal equipoise, and there finding finale solace and contentment in Self as Source. In other words, the male and the female inner aspects joining to become one, is the very method to obtain eternal life.

Additionally the word "befitting" is referring to the knowledge or gnosis of the *Truth* that we are the actual fragmentation of the Creator Beings, or that we are in actuality God/Goddess. This Truth has all of the Creation (Entirety) standing in awe, and humble acknowledgement, with complete acceptance and peace of mind, in an eternal embrace of tranquil love and grace. This rest represents the return of the All to the One. Additionally, when it says that the disciples will proceed to their repose; (repose: complete rest or the resting place of their true home, also represents their fullness as Creator beings in the beginning), this is their (*your*) rightful place as the Eternal Twinships of the Most High Parent Entity; God/Goddess at Source, as Source.

The following statement sums it up very well, *"For the end is where the beginning is. Blessed is the person who stands at repose in the beginning. And that person will be acquainted with the end and will not taste death." ~ Gospel of Thomas*

Quoting Jesus and empowered by Truth and Gnosis, I paraphrase with great compassion and conviction, *"The end is where the beginning is"* how profound and sublime indeed. For, *"you have come from the Light-Kingdom, so there you will return."* We simply need to embrace or claim this as our birthright and become the aspect and frequency of the portion of the Zodiac creation wheel that we represent. (Each Twin Flame couple represents a house of the Zodiac). Again, I emphasize a very important part of the ascension process is discovering and integrating a higher awareness of all aspects of Self. Becoming aware of your lineage (soul family) or creational frequency ray is very much apart of this.

Take this perspective to heart and feel the impact of the words found in the Pistis Sophia, stating, "…*The 12 (Twin) Saviors will save the world.*" What I strongly sense and feel is that this means the 24 eternals and their emanations (i.e. 144,000 Children of Light) will be incarnate and become the Teachers of Teachers at this time in history. I will also be presenting information about the role of the twin flames, in preceding chapters, which is becoming more and more of a powerful catalyst for the transformation to the 5th dimension. There is a very great deal of information in the Pistis Sophia, which is extremely revealing. I was completely amazed at how much it paralleled my discovery and interpretation of what I had been guided to recall and reveal. I had actually never before read the Pistis Sophia I was elated to see the wisdom and greater understanding echoed there, which I had always sensed through my being

There literally is so much interesting information in the Pistis Sophia, rather than try to cover it all or reproduce it here, you can reference it on my web site www.gnosisunveiled.com and appreciate its fullness.

I had discovered the Pistis Sophia on the Internet shortly after I began this project. To my pleasant surprise my understanding was almost exactly portrayed word for word. This was incredibly inspiring to the work, but most importantly, it basically confirmed my life and existence. Yet again, apparently, I still needed to address that personal doubt. Some of my spiritual friends had Previously lovingly called me "Doubting Thomas" which may have been rather fitting after all.

It is also very noteworthy to mention that when I discovered the Pistis Sophia on the Internet in 1997, I had a very profound prompting from Spirit to write this book, and that it was actually time to begin it. I was doing some journaling and sketching when I was contemplating beginning it when a major synchronicity happened. I was drawing out my understanding of the creational model, which began with a small diagram that depicted the essence of the core of creation. That afternoon I was searching the Internet for some Gnostic Scripture information and the very first thing that came up was a link to, "the Books of the

Savior", another set of books I had never seen or heard of yet. Much to my utter amazement and absolute surprise there on the first page of this document was the diagram I had just drawn earlier that day. What a profound synchronistic cue.

Some other points I wish to touch on, which also have strong validations of our divinity, are found in the Gnostic Scriptures. One of the most significant is the existence of the "Light-Power" or Merkaba; as a garment of light, as a descending dove. This is another aspect of its divine nature. Each phrase has a different meaning or purpose, however all represent the Merkaba as a vehicle for consciousness to travel interdimensionally, as well as penetrate time and space. The reference to the dove is somewhat of a different means of consciousness bi location. An example of this is found in the Bible, when the FATHER descended upon Jesus at his baptism in the river Jordon, in the form of the dove. This is referred to is an overshadowing or a blending of additional consciousness matrices with ones own soul. There are several variations of this, the most common is know as; a soul walk-in. Additionally, a soul may be braided by several master souls at the same; this was the case with Jesus.

The following is some of the most profound excerpts from Pistis Sophia that reinforce and validate my inner understanding of what it is to be aware of ones ascended or eternal consciousness, i.e. the nature of our soul essence.

*Jesus said, "Don't you realize that you and the angels and Archangels and the gods and the Lords and the Rulers, and all the invisibles, as well as those of the middle, and those belonging to the region of the Right and indeed all the emanations of the Light in all their glory, are from the same essence and the same substance and that you all come for from the same mixture."*

"It was at the command of the First Mystery, that the mixture was constrained to bring forth the great emanations of the Light, with all their glory. According to the wealth of the One and Only Ineffable they were required to purify themselves from the mixture and from themselves. You are therefore the chosen essence that has been elected from the Treasury of Light. You are the essence from those in the region of the Right and from all the invisibles and from the Rulers too. But they have not known suffering as you have. Neither have they experienced changes from region to region, nor have they torn themselves away (projected fragmentation's from the oversoul) so as to be poured into various kinds of bodies as you have. They have not experienced affliction or great suffering (of the many embodiments) such, as you have known when you were poured from one kind of body into another kind in this world.

But even after these sufferings you have wrestled with your selves and striven until you have renounced the whole world and its matter. You did not leave off seeking, until you had found the Mysteries belonging to the Kingdom of Light, which purified and made you into exceeding pure and refined light." ~ Pistis Sophia

# The 24 Disciples
(Wisdom / Gnosis)

The number 12 is well known in the mystic schools and metaphysical circles as a divine number with a myriad of implications and correlations, ranging from the 12 signs of the Zodiac, the 12 hours of the day, the 12 Immortals of the Greek Pantheon, the 12 tribes of Israel; to the 12 Disciples of Christ. All these Twelves are very suggestive of the divinity of creation. I have never found that much information about why it is so prominent in terms of the number value itself. From what I have and will demonstrate here, it will become more obvious and definitive as to the significance of the number.

Several other sources have in recent year's channeled information about the first emanation of the 12 original races, which is the primary reason behind the vast amount of information carried down through history concerning the number 12.

The 12 hours of the day have a key to a deeper understanding. The day light hours are the reciprocal of 12 opposite hours. The night hours, which are the opposite of the day light hours on the other side of the planet represent the 24 hours of the day. Here we find another example of the two sides of the polarity coin. This integral component of existence reflects the higher levels of creation emanating from the 12 male creator beings and the 12 female creator beings.

From the depiction put forth here you can see where the number 24 has its significance, the Creator Beings, who literally created or where responsible for everything in the universe, from galaxies to quasars, ethereal realms to souls, from planets to animals, and molecules to beings of various corporeal forms, using their Spirit and essence to animate consciousness, patterned it all after the original template.

The 24 Creator Beings are the vibrational representation of the 12 Father figure aspects (i.e. Parent Entities) that birthed their respective branch of existence.

The pattern or matrix of creation actually carries the vibration of both 12 and 24 and their frequency essence throughout the entire creation. However, the balance or harmonious expression of that energy is more accurately or intensely portrayed in the expression of the male and female counterparts connected to each parent entity. In other words, the personification of these 12 primal frequency rays are imbued into each reality or perceived existence by means of the actual galvanization of each unique creational counterpane expressed in human form. (An energetic form of the 24 frequencies can be seen expressed in the Appendix on page 649 and 654.)

Thus, I present to you that my inner knowing of the time of Jesus and his Disciples, was slightly different from what was recorded. There was a total of 24 main Disciples, 12 males and 12 females. The divine pattern of creation was fully expressed at this transitional time in history, with each of the Creator Beings present at that time. The misrepresentation of the information was largely due to the overall suppression of femininity or the nature of the Goddess, more expressly was the denial of the strength of the emotions, and the sacredness of the human being in all its qualities and traits.

The power of the intellect, strength, courage or show-of-might was the ruling force at those times, for it was a warring world where the strong survived and ruled, while the weak fell or served. Therefore, at this time the infusion of the truth of equality in the genders, as well as the reciprocation of the polarities in a balanced holism, comprised the message. The introduction of the Christ consciousness to the planetary awareness was through the understanding that Christ consciousness was fundamentally the realization and perception that we, as divine spiritual beings are truly both qualities of the polarity energies of creation personified in a singly manifested form, i.e. each human being is vibrationally both male and female.

The highest or fullest expression of the Body/Mind system of a conscious sentient is the galvanization or conjoined embodiment of both intellect and emotions. Christ is the complete identification of the combined expression of the two qualities of the full essence of existence. To be a Christed being is to fully embrace each polarity and become an integrated One, from the two primordial essences or faculties. Again, this message was demonstrated and delivered by an example of this awareness. The relationship between Mary Magdalene, and the Master Jesus together was a divine expression of the original Twinships, for they where the embodiment of the 1st created Creator beings; the *First Mystery*.

The Gnostic Scriptures give a very clear understanding of their relationship:

> "Three women always used to walk with the Lord – Mary his Mother, his sister and the Magdalene, who was his companion. For Mary was the name of his sister and his mother, and it is the name of his (true) partner." In addition, "The Wisdom who is called barren wisdom is the mother of the angels, and the companion of the Lord, who is called Mary Magdalene." Moreover "The Lord Jesus loved her more than all the rest of the disciples, and he used to kiss her on the mouth more often than the rest. They asked him, 'why do you love her more than all the rest?'"

Jesus response was a parable in jest; saying she is woman and you are men.

The second quoted verse refers to how Mary is attributed to the female Creator aspect, overall known as Sophia or Wisdom. I would additionally like to present the postulation, which to date is purely of my own personal recall of those days, regarding what I expressed above as the patterning of the creation matrix. I have come to understand several significant methods or aspects as to how many of us on the spiritual path have had strong recall of being there at the time of Christ. The most prominent way that all the 24 Creators where present or represented then was through oversoul overshadowing, thought that is not to say that there was not the complete expression of several direct incarnations. We will be discovering a little known secret of the deeper expression of the twin aspects of creation in part two.

The relevance to multiple divine incarnations is to some extent further supported by one channeled book, authored by Joseph Whitfield, called the Secret Treasures of El Dolrado. It states that each of the Apostles was an incarnation of one of the Ascended Masters; he details six with some of their main lifetimes throughout earth's history. These were six of the most notorious Masters, these are the Masters over the 12 rays of creation, further emphasizing that each ray constitutes the primary virtues or characteristics of the 12 races.

It is interesting to note that the New Testament in Matthew chapter 19, verse 28 we find a reflection of what the Gnostic Scriptures has regarding the authority of the Apostles and the initiation process that Jesus re-gained in Egypt. The word *regeneration* is the same word that Edgar Cayce uses regarding those that will return in the end times. Matthew emphasizes this in relating that Jesus said, *"Verily I say unto you, that ye which have followed me, in the regeneration when the Son of man shall sit in the throne of his glory, ye also shall sit upon twelve thrones, judging the twelve tribes of Israel."*

As we can see, the reference to the twelve, is a predominate theme, though only half of the greater equation.

It is especially significant to note that the book the Hiram Key by Christopher Knight and Robert Lomas, describes the discovery of a secret chamber under King Herod's Temple. According to several ancient letters and notes from the Knights Templar (the first Freemasons) states that the original secret books of Moses, which apparently had instructions to be hid away, was found on an altar, which was encircled with the 12 Zodiac signs in mosaic stone.

It is becoming evident that there are several key pieces (i.e. number codes) needed to complete the greater puzzle of the grand cosmic clock, revealing the understanding that there is a super science or meta-physics of creation. On the surface humanity has retained a glimpse of what the gears of the clock looks like. Although the comprehension of what it means when the hour hand strikes midnight is not just a function of knowing that the bells are chiming. One must have knowledge of what each minute is and how that relates to the whole.

The following is further evidence supporting that Jesus was looking for both males and females when choosing his disciples.

THE 7TH SEAL

*"I will choose you 1 out of 1000 and 2 out of 10,000 and they will stand at rest by being one and the same"* ~ Gospel of Thomas (This refers to the locating of the 12 of the 24 Twin Flames.)

## Bridal Chamber - A Great Mystery Revealed
### (Gnosis)

The Bridal Chamber in the days of Jesus was the bedroom chamber where the Bride and the Groom, after having been married, would go to consecrate their union to one another. The act of joining together as one flesh was the sacred blending together and bonding of the male and the female.

This term was chosen to represent the final stage and the completed state of being (the marriage of the inner male and female), which was achieved through the entire procedure or ceremony of the bestowal of the *"Five Seals"*. The ritual was a five-step process, which resulted in the total transformation into an Ascended Being. The five steps were also referred to as the *"Five Trees of Paradise"*, which was a take off on the story or analogy to two trees in the Garden of Eden. Each step had a specific attribute or quality, which would produce a required state of awareness or balance in the body/mind system of the initiate. The general content of the steps are as follows.

The first step was the Baptismal by water, which would purify the emotional body, releasing or identifying any blocks that needed to be processed and removed in order to be clear and open to receive.

The second step was the Baptismal by fire, or chrism, which would cleanse and purify the mental body, again releasing or identifying blocks. Blocks are issues and limiting belief systems which bind or inhibited the natural flow of energy in the body/mind system. An open and harmonious relationship between these two bodies needed to exist in order to be balanced and have awareness in all levels of the body/mind system.

The Third step was the Eucharist, which was the receiving of the Gnosis or the Body and the Blood of Christ. This is also representative of the Grail for it is the bread (earth) and wine (water) that are alchemically balanced as the body and emotions in the previous steps. This represented the full understanding of the nature of the soul and true perfect human being, which meant that the individual was capable of far greater feats than what was normally expected from a mere human, 3rd dimensionally and interdimensionally.

The Fourth step was the Ransom, which was the actual implementation and activation of the light body or Merkaba. This was referred to as *"putting on the Garment of Light"*. It was called Ransom because it was what would redeem the soul from the material coil/realm or cycle of karmic incarnations.

The Fifth and final step was the *"Bridal Chamber"*, which was two-fold, one was the act of marring or joining together the two polarity aspects of self into one, the male and the female as, the left and the right. This conscious awareness and integration produced a state of being enabling the second half of the process. The second part was the making of *"the inside like the outside and the upper like the lower"*. This was the reunification with the higher self or the true self in awareness and actuality. Then the individual would become the Ascended Hu-man being that it truly is. This was the direct result of a full Merkaba activation and total integration within the body/mind system of all aspects of Self, above and below. Thus, becoming an actual Christ Conscious Being, capable of total mastery over this 3rd dimensional reality with a myriad of natural God-like talents.

What is extremely interesting regarding all the inferences to the process and the actual state of becoming Christ-like in the Gnostic Scriptures is that we have only a few remnants of it in the New Testament. For example, *"you shall do greater things than I (Jesus)"* and *"when you say move to the mountain it will move"* essentially stating that literally anything is possible.

Although the references to this in the Gnostic Scriptures are more descriptive and clear, with one of the best examples being:

*"Anyone who will work my mysteries will be set before the first unbegotten ones"* and *"Should not all people who posses all things know themselves utterly?*

Now, if some do not *(truly)* know themselves, they will not have the use of what they posses, but those who have learned *(the Gnosis)* about themselves will do so." *(Unbegotten is the parent entity.)*

The very best phrase in my opinion is this saying from the Gospel of Thomas, saying # 22:

"Jesus saw little ones nursing. He said to his disciples, 'What these little ones resemble are those who enter the Kingdom,' *(a perfect natural internal balance)* they said to him, "So shall we enter the Kingdom by being little ones? He said, "When you make the two one and make the inside like the outside and the outside like the inside and the above like the below, and you make the male and the female one and the same, so that the male might not be male nor the female be female¢h¢hen you will enter the Kingdom.'"

In addition, "Many are standing at the door, only the solitaries will enter the Bridal Chamber." Therefore, with all this preponderance of evidence one must agree absolute *balance* is paramount; as well as a complete understanding of the polarization of self in your perception of reality.

Moreover, here are some of the specifics of the first few initiations, but most significantly notice the metaphors.

The Gnostic Gospel of Phillip has this to say, "Soul and Spirit are constituted of fire and water, and a son *(/daughter)* of the bridal chamber is constituted of fire and water and light. Fire is chrism *(essential oil used in ceremony)* - light is fire; but I do not mean worldly fire, which has no form, but another kind of fire *(frequency and vibration)*, whose appearance is white. It is beautifully luminous and bestows beauty."

Also from the Gospel of Phillip we find another representation, "When we are 'reborn' by the Holy Spirit, we are born by the Anointed *(Christed)* through two things, we are anointed by Spirit *(Christed by the goddess aspect)* and when we were born *(/reborn)* we were joined *(with Spirit as the Breath)*. No one can see himself in the water or in a mirror without light. For this reason, it is necessary to baptize with two things; light and

THE 7TH SEAL

*water. And light means chrism"* (This was also symbolic in the ceremony of the two aspects of the perfected self; male/light/oil - soul/mind/electric and female/water/spirit - feelings/magnetic.)

This is also reflected later in the Gospel of Phillip, *"By water and fire the entire place (all the bodies) is sanctified, the visible (elements of it) by the visible, the hidden by the hidden. Some (elements) are hidden by the visible; there is water within water, and there is fire within chrism."* (The oil of chrism is visible, but the frequency of the oil, which purifies and effects the bodies, are beyond the physical and are hidden.)

It states in several sources (i.e. The Aquarian Gospels of Jesus Christ) that Jesus traveled to may other countries teaching and learning their traditions and knowledge. It is quite possible that some of these practices came from the Egyptian Mystery schools.

*"The Rulers do not see those who have put on the perfect light, one will put on the light in a mystery, through the act of joining." - Gospel of Phillip*

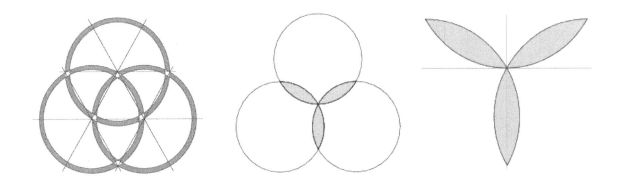

It is most interesting to see what shapes can be derived from the intersection of three circles. This can represent "the two becoming one." Mother and Father create Child.

**[These simple shapes would become paramount code symbols and messages or icons of the divine stories]**

# Merkaba – "Wheel within Wheels"
### (Gnosis)

The Merkaba is three-dimensional star tetrahedral with counter rotating fields of electro-magnetic energy, which surrounds all life forms, from galaxies to planets, and from humans to molecules. It is the *"Wheels within Wheels"* referenced in many sacred scriptures, literally a non-linear energetic vessel for inter-dimensional travel. It is

also referred to as the *"Garment of Light"*. We will be learning much more about this powerful shape and its overall energy pattern throughout this book.

Leonardo da Vinci was very studied in the sacred sciences. It is clear that he understood the reciprocal nature of creation evidenced is his art and the following statement: *"Art without Science is nothing."*

*We will discover a great deal about the esoteric value and nature of this symbol as we progress in the deeper or "Greater Mysteries".*

The 7th Seal

# Bridal Chamber Ceremony Recital
## (Gnosis)

The following ceremony is from the finale ritual for being born again into Ascension. The excerpt is from the Gnostic Scriptures entitled; *The Holy Book of the Great Invisible Spirit*, also known as the <u>Book of the Egyptians</u>!

In very truth O Living Water, O Child of Child,
   (Followed by a recital of vowels of names of all Glories, perhaps toning)

EEEEthOOOO YYYY OOOO AAAAth
   (a total of 24 lines of similar text follows here)

Existent Epsilon (five) forever unto eternity.

In very truth IEO AIO in the heart.

You are what you are. You are who you are.
   (Eternal)

This great name of yours is upon me, O Self-Originate that lacks nothing and is free, O invisible unto all but me.
   (Perfect Divine Human)

For what being can comprehend you by speech or praise.
   (Gnosis)

Having myself become acquainted.
   (Passed all initiations)

I have girded myself and come to dwell in an armor of loveliness and light.
   (The garment of light)

I have become Illuminous.

For the Mother was there, because of the fair beauty of loveliness.
   (Joining with the Spirit)

For this reason, I have stretched forth my hands.
   (Doing the Merkaba            )

I have been formed within the orbit of the riches of the Light.
   (Increasing the Ball of Light or frequency in the Heart)

For it is within my bosom, bestowing form upon the various engendered beings by unreproachable light.
   (Expanded sphere, out beyond the Merkaba)

I shall truly declare your praise, for I have comprehended you.
   (Had the hidden revealed)

It is you, O Jesus, O Eternal Omega, Eternal Epsilon, O Jesus, O Eternity.

You are my realm of repose.
   (Stand fully aware as Divine)

Being without form that dwells among those (also) without form.
   (An Eternal in the invisible realm)

Raising a Human Being by whom you will sanctify me, into your life according to your ineffable name.
   (Ascension to the Divine Perfect form)

For this reason the fragrance of life is within me.
   (The flower of life as the Entirety)

For it has been mixed with baptismal water to serve as a prototype for all rulers.
   (Example for all)

So that in your company I might have life in the peace of the saints.
   (Become one of the Eternals)

O' eternally existent.

In very truth.

"He who gains victory over others is strong, but he who gains victory over himself is all powerful." ~ Lao Tzu

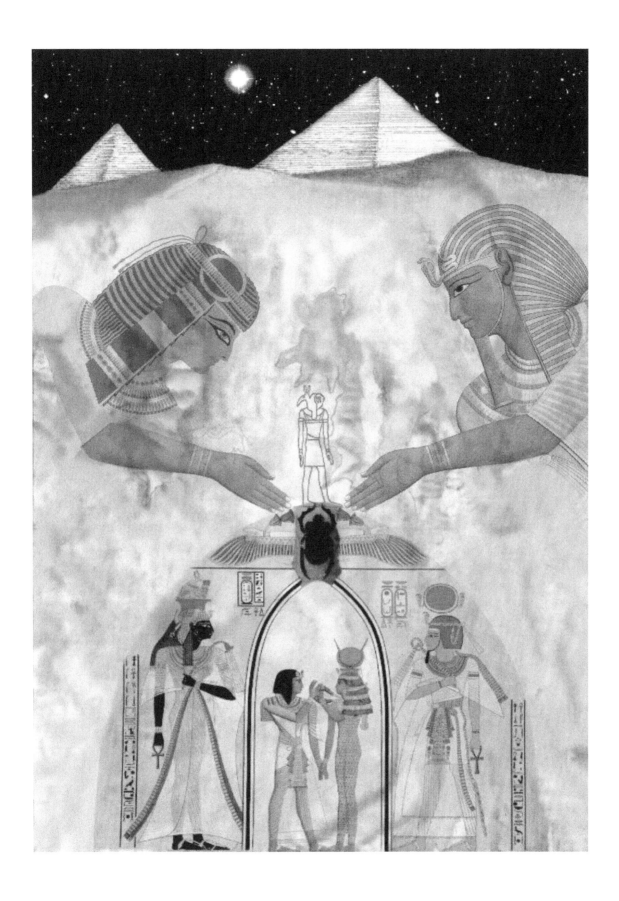

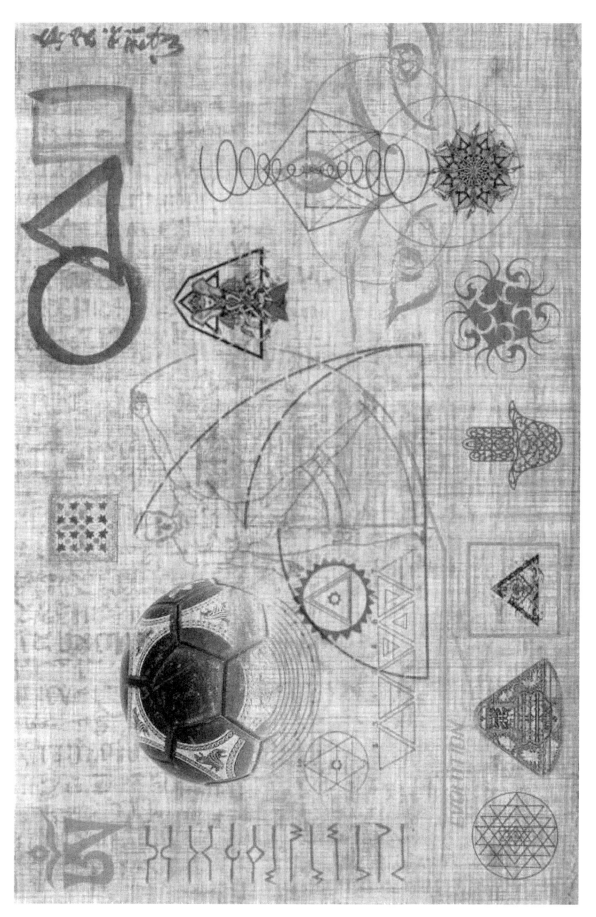

# 5th Foundational Creation
(Story Line/Gnosis)

The 5th Foundational prophecy as given by Cosmo (as I have sensed it too) is a forecast pertaining to the setting the stage or laying the energetic groundwork for the creation of the 5th generational universe.

The 5th Foundational prophecy is multifaceted, although the primary essence running through it is the single focused, full embrace of the Goddess within all of creation, thus the name or theme of the prophecy: "Return of the Goddess". This universal movement is all about the return to a holistic or shall I say, a wholistic acceptance of the ALL as ONE.

The prophecy itself is an overall measure of what is occurring trans-universally, that will energetically entrain the creation of the 5th universe. What does all this mean? There are several levels to the full extent of universes, which occupy the same space but are all at different frequencies. There are those that are outside of one another and those that are inside of one another and yet invisible to each other. Overall, there is a natural flow of energy permeating throughout the creational genesis. As a continual ebb and flow of the great cosmic breath that unites all existence through Spirit, blown outward as far as intended, now inhales in preparation for the next creational step. All that has been collectively experienced will be utilized in creating greater expressions of perfection.

A universal prayer or creed honoring our connection with the One, might start something like this, *"Our Father who art in Heaven and our Mother who art in Earth, blessed be thy soul and spirit, which reside in me, for thy Kingdom IS come."* As well as, rather than, "I AM that I AM", a more wholistic, "I AM that WE are".

There are deeper implications and meanings to this movement, some of which will become more evident as things continue to unfold. The fundamental tenant though is less patriarchal hierarchy and over intellectualize approach, to the extent that compassion and love have suffered and in some cases utterly fallen by the wayside. Again, realize the correlation of,"as above, so below". What occurs on one level is often a reflection or reaction from another. We are literally ALL are a reflection of Source, collectively calling back our original creational out breath.

Another way of perceiving this shift in somewhat greater detail, is that all dimensions, in all universal creations are moving up a step or level, so to speak on the stairway to heaven, or the pathway back to source. So what do you suppose will happen at the last step, at the top or pearly gates? It would make sense that some beings are at the doorstep waiting to return home already. Although, in order for this to happen something must take place first, in terms of energy, as this is the extent of everything. What has been shown to me is a procession of souls, as it where, a sort of backward-stepping or reverse engineering. When you are dealing with a natural language, a universal system of intelligent self-generating creations, which is in effect an evolutionary process of all energy returning to source, it will naturally follow the same universal laws, which it unfolded to.

Therefore, what this all means is, or what must happen is a reformation of all male/female energy, since all souls were created both male/female in the holographic image as God/Goddess. A reunification must occur before stepping through heavens gate. This will undoubtedly take some time; although many transformational processes are speeding up; largely due to the principal of gaining momentum with critical mass or the one hundredth and one monkey theory.

For the sake of simplicity, the one hundredth monkey theory is based on an experiment that proved that intelligence or conscious awareness is passed by a type of consciousness osmosis. In other words, the hundredth monkey phenomenon refers to a sudden spontaneous and mysterious leap of consciousness achieved when an allegedly "critical mass" point is reached. Stated plainly, once 100 people understand and accept anything as true and practical, the 101$^{st}$ will get it by second nature.

The Grand Universal cycle, which is coming to completion, is at the same time the beginning of the next paramount genesis of the 5$^{th}$ generation universe, thus the Fifth world or the fifth root race, with all the significant values or expressions of five.

It is interesting to note that both the Mayans and the Egyptians record four other worlds or epochs, in the case of the Egyptians the average recorded length of these epochs is 26,000 years. Both civilizations calendars end in 2012. The Hopis also follow this same drum beat, with prophecies of the next world to come being an expression of the Rainbow Nation when all people of all colors are united into one harmonies beat.

The following excerpts from The Book of the Savior (Pistis Sophia) reinforce what has just been put forth in this chapter.

*Jesus said, "The dissolution of the universe will come after the number of perfect souls is completed in the Mystery for which the universe arose has been finished. Dissolving the world, when the universe will be raised up. All those who have received the Mysteries of the Ineffable will reign as Kings with me and sit on my Right hand and Left hand in my Kingdom. Then I will spend a thousand years, according to the years of light, reigning over all the emanations of Light."*

> "Once the number of perfect souls is completed, then the Mystery of the First Mystery will be completed, on whose account the whole universe arose. I am that Mystery. From that hour onwards, no one will be able to enter into the Light and no one will be able to go forth, from when the time is completed. I will set fire to the world, so that the Aeons and the Veils and the Firmaments and the whole world with all its material and all mankind which exists at the time, may be purified." Mary Magdalene asked, "Will all of matter be destroyed then or not?" Jesus replied, "Every nature, every formation and every creature which exists, one with another, will be resolved again into their original roots. The nature of matter, for instance, will be resolved into its nature alone. Let him that has ears to hear, listen. However before that all occurs, the faith and the Mysteries will be even more fully revealed. And as I have previously mentioned, many souls will be coming back, by means of the circuits, in different bodies, and some of them will be people, who heard my teachings during this lifetime." ∽ Pistis Sophia

This is extremely revealing and very frank indeed, stating plainly that we are the energy of creation, embodied in these physical souls, returning over and over again. It also states that once the perfect number of souls is complete, namely the 144,000 oversoul, then this Universe Generation will be complete, and all energy will be recalled or purified for the next genesis.

Additionally, from the Secret Book of John, reinforcing the veracity of what is being put forth here concerning the nature of our soul's existence.

> Jesus said, "I say to you, everyone who will receive the Mystery of the Ineffable, even though they are human, living in the world, they will tower above, all the angels, Archangels, Lords, Gods, Givers of Light, Pure Ones, Tri-Powers, Forefathers, Invisibles, and even above the great Invisible Forefather. And even though he may be a man of the world, he will tower above the emanations from the Treasury of Light. He will exalt himself above the Mixture completely. Even though he is a man of the world he will rule with me in my Kingdom, for although he is a man living in this world, he is a King in the Light. He may be a man living in the world, but he is not of the world. I say to you, Amen. That man is I and I am that man." ∽ The Secret Book of John

THE 7TH SEAL

This is also very telling, indeed.

*"I asked the Savior, Lord, would all the souls then be brought safely into pure light? These things are difficult to explain to the many, except those who are from the immovable Race (Eternal), or, in other words, those on whom the Spirit of life will descend and whom it will empower. These will be saved and become **Perfect** and be worthy of the greatness and become purified in that place (State) from all. Then, they will have no other care except incorruption alone and they will direct their attention from then on, without anger or envy or jealousy or desire or greed for anything. They will not be affected by anything, except the state of being in the flesh, which they will bear while looking expectantly for the time when the Receivers of Light will come to meet them. Such a one will be worthy of the imperishable eternal life and the calling, for they will endure everything, so that they may finish the good fight and inherit eternal life."* ~ The Secret Book of John

# First Wavers
### (Story Line - Gnosis)

The First Ascension, which is spoken about in both the New Testament and the Book of Mormon, refers to the Elect who are the Chosen ones that will do Gods work in the end times. This has also been referred to as the first wave of three. What does all this actually mean? The Elect are those who have incarnated aware that they are here to assist at this time of awakening. The Ascension or raising of consciousness regarding what is taking place at this current time has been in preparation for thousand of years. The Elect have reincarnated over and over again refining their awareness and leaving clues that would be found and utilized during these End Times. For in truth it is a beginning more than it is an end, and in this understanding the **chosen** are really those individuals who choose to assist the process of teaching and guiding humanity into the next dimension.

The first wave will be the *'Teachers of the Teachers'*, by which the second wave will be reached and readied in mind and body. The desire is for as many souls as possible to become aware of what is truly taken place in this lifetime. The first wave also has a timetable associated with it. This schedule was partially laid out in the book of revelations, where it says there will be seven trumpets that will sound, also referred to as *the opening of seven seals*. At the end of which, the first wave will have been completed. The first of these trumpets sounded in March 5th, of 1995, when the planets in the sky arranged themselves into a Star of David or Merkaba.

This was also accompanied by the arrival of the comet Hale-bopp. Though the exact time this actually occurred or was counted as the strongest energy wise was when it was closest to earth, which was on 23rd of March. Also occurring during this time; *"a third of the world burned"*, this was the exact quote from Revelations.

This could be seen as the massive fires around the globe; from Australia to South America, and a few countries in between, was another prophecy revealed.

The second Trumpet was the meteorite that struck Greenland in Dec. 1997. This was the fulfilling of; *"and the sea would turn red and the mountains would burn with fire and the sun nor moon would not shine"*.

This was actually seen in Greenland, the mountaintops looked like they where on fire with a massive red glow all around them. Although, the sea was actually missed by the blow, the ice, which makes up most of the landmass there, turned red. The last effect that could be seen there was on the atmosphere, where the dust and smoke was so thick that it caused the sun and moon not shine for 3 days.

The third trumpet to sound was predicted to occur sometime in 2001. We have seen several motion pictures about the very nature of this Trumpet. Perhaps a meteorite can be expected, relating to the verse in Revelations, which says that; *"a third of the worlds water turn bitter"*, this is believed to be the effect of the blast on the continent of America, causing the lakes and rivers, and possibly the underground tributaries to be polluted. Although this could certainly be the fore seen state of the condition of most of the drinking water currently available in the United States.

This would be the wake-up call of all wake-up calls, with many people turning to God. Nevertheless, the Teachers and Teachers of Teachers will answer the call and many people will be ready to listen. This is not to instill fear in the hearts and minds of the readers, because all these events, regardless to the degree of catastrophic events in the years to come will be made clear for those who have eyes to see and ears to hear. In other words, when you open your heart to the truth, and the light, and the way you will be guided to be in the right place at the right time, and in this way will be protected or safe. This could also be the expected return of Planet X, or the 12th Planet that has actually been sited, which is on its way here. According to Zacharias Stichen, the Author of "The Earth Chronicles", the Sumerians have clay tablets depicting the solar system with a larger planetary body in orbit where the asteroid belt is. They state that this occurs every 3,600 years. There are reports that I have heard from a secret source (They don't want there named used) stating that top-secret government officials know that this Planet X is coming and with an Asteroid in tow.

It really doesn't matter what experiences await us, whether they will ultimately be allowed to affect this planet and it's divine evolution or not is entirely up to how many people are making the grades in the required shift in consciousness that is taking place now. There are literally hundreds of thousands of spiritual people on the planet, believing in humanity and her ability to make a difference. We simple must hold the intention of connecting with one another to form an alignment of the divine will and we will move mountains.

When you choose the *path of ascension* and/or *the way of the dimensional shift*, a great many things begin to change in your life. This is a path many being's souls are already on, and this is a journey full of personal experiences and incredible self-discovery; of which testimonials certainly are not lacking. If you are not already certain that this is a path that you are on, you need only open your heart and with the purest of intention and desire ask God, your Guardian Angels or your Guides, whatever your higher power is, to give you a sign that will confirm or show you your truth. All that is required to make the shift towards greater understanding is to come from a space of sincerity and determination to open your heart to unconditional love and radiate compassion. Continue to watch your thoughts and choose love in all that you do. You will certainly see signs that the universe is smiling on you.

To those of you who are on this path already, what I wish to encourage you to do today or right now, is to make a conscious choice to claim your birthright and not only shift but ascend in frequency to the divine state of being that you are innately an intricate part of. For the whole is not complete without all its parts, therefore simply choose to BE the IS in whol-is-m. *Remember that it is not in the doing, but the **being** that makes the difference.* Many things in this book will assist you in perceiving the awareness of an ascended consciousness.

> Jesus' disciples asked, "Tell us how the end will come?" Jesus said, "Have you found the beginning then, that you are already looking for the end. You see, the end is where the beginning is. The one who stands at the beginning, that one will know the end and not taste death." ~ Gospel of Thomas

THE 7TH SEAL

*As we watch for the next signs of the times and await the next Trumpet could it be possible that we are now receiving the opening of the Seals aspect of the Revelations prophecy? This is a very different kind of portend for change, as we shall see.*

# Twin Flames Reunite
### *(Story Line - Gnosis)*

Lately we have heard more and more about the Twin Flames coming together and doing great work on the path of highest light. This is becoming more and more prominent because of several reasons. The most obvious is due to the fact that we are approaching the end of the grand cycle. Although Twin Flame souls have been helping each other and working together since the beginning, it was more common for the actual interaction here on earth for the counterpart to come as a spirit guide. This counterpart was working from the other side to assist in guiding the respective individual to their highest path, an ultimate return home to fully reunite.

The way the oversoul transformation use to occur was in a singular fashion, when a soul returned to the oversoul level it did so through the same gender. In other words, after the oversoul created the soul, it was still male and female; following the laws of this genesis creation, it then split. Therefore, the return (oversoul transformation) would be the half of the soul returning or transforming back into the parent polarity it represented. (i.e. The male soul expression, even though experiencing feminine lives, would upon its completion of lessons and experiences, energetically return to the masculine half of the oversoul or Father soul.)

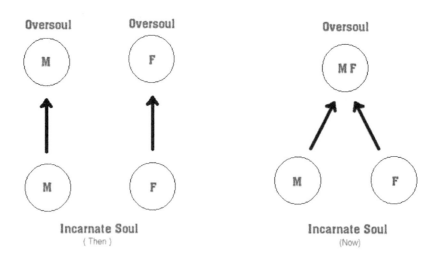

One of the most powerful energetic shifts that occurred helping in this process has been the planetary alignment of 5/5/2000. This brought great internal transformation around seeking the sacred marriage of the Divine beloved within. This step is mandatory for the completion of the Twin Flames sacred marriage with the Divine complement without.

At critical times in history Twin Flames incarnate together to assist in a more powerful manner. This is the case now, with the shift right around the corner with the end of the Mayan and Egyptian calendars as December 12th, 2012. Recently there has been a less obvious aspect of the change in the way Twin Flames are going through the oversoul process. This is in preparation for the higher-level change that the completion of the grand cycle is bringing about.

It is now apparent to me that the way that all this is occurring is that the Creator Beings are rejoining and all the children are reuniting on down through the levels. And when a transformation occurs the parents are now joined so the child's soul needs to return as one combined energy. This is necessary to adhere to the original energy matrix, which is patterned by the Creator Beings. This is taking place because as the generations of the Divine Twinships returning to source, they will be returning to the Parent Entity as they where originally created, as one being, both male and female. This is thus requiring greater assistance from each aspect of the respective twin counterparts, helping one another to become whole again in the higher dimensions.

The unification of the divine Twinships has already begun. There is confirmation from several channeled sources that the Ascended Masters who occupy the offices of the Cohan of the Seven Rays, have moved up to the next level of service /vibration. Thus leaving their previous seats vacant, which are now being occupied by both the Male and a Female Twinship combined.

This whole process is in preparation for the beginning of the creation of the 5th universe genesis creation. This creation will have a completely reorganized dispensation with entirely new Creator Beings and most likely an all new theme; the theme of this current universe creation being that of a Polarity expression, who knows what is next? Cosmos says that several adjustments have been made of late to assist in this over all process that will enable more souls to ascend. Essentially, the prime policy of non-interference has been relaxed to some extent allowing more help than ever before from the higher realms. One of the most interesting changes is that the souls who do not make the shift in this life time (leaving only one lifetime opportunity left in this reality) may be transported to previous time lines or other simultaneous universes, to continue their growth process and integration there.

This supports what I have always sensed or believed, in that; the planet earth in its 3rd dimensional nature would no longer exist after this shift. It seems that the higher dimensions will also be making a shift up one level, so to speak, on the overall return to source. This is so that as each level is stepped up one level, the lowest level would be wrapped up energetically in the gathering up of the energy of its existence.

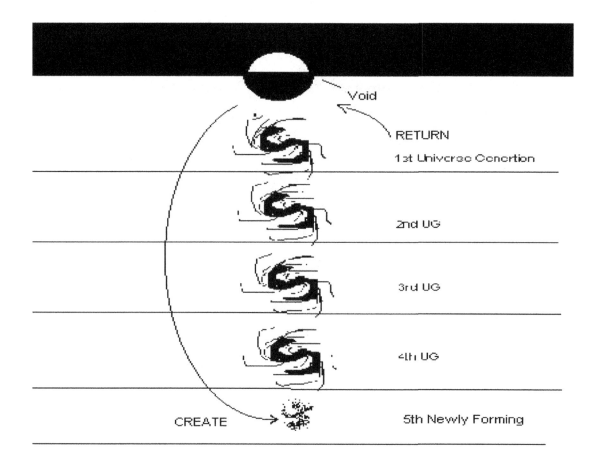

I also believe this is how the Planetary Logos is returning to re-unit with her Twin aspect, from our early story about Sanat Kumara and Sophia. It is quite possible that the creation of the next universe generation will be a simultaneous exchange of energy, in that as one level is returned here, the first level will be created there. I have speculated with my friend Cosmo who concurs with my postulation. In other words, the Creator beings are laying the foundation of the next Genesis Universe experiment concurrently with the culmination of this creation.

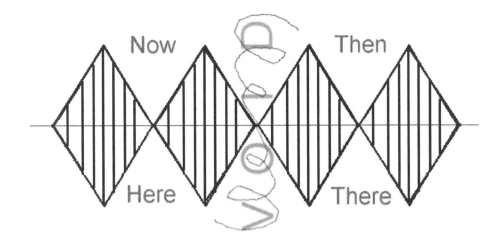

Cosmo has shared much about his experiences concerning the greater transformations that are taking place at this time, including his wisdom regarding the extra-dimensional awareness and conscious travels that he has made. He has elaborated on the nature of the visions and awareness that many have been receiving regarding the existence of a mirror universe or creation.

It is the exact opposite of here. The reciprocal energy counterpart of all that exists here is reflected there. Everything that is thought here is created there and visa versa. He also speaks of parallel realities that we share with additional counter parts that are just one phase shift away from our present reality. These are trans-dimensions that are a form of extra energy that is mirrored into the spaces in between, so to speak. There are four time-lines, if you will that are directly connect to ours. You as your earthly identity, are on each one, with very similar life's and makeup, though slightly different paths or out comes. Each one is about 150 years ahead of the previous. Cosmos says he is from the first, so 600 years in the future. This world/trans-dimension is called Utelica. He says there are many who have come back on a mission to assist in our full awakening and first contact with the Galactic family, as there are better ways to accomplish these transformations, than what they had done. He says that time travel has been perfected for some time and that in the future I have traveled to the distant past, to none other than Egypt.

THE 7TH SEAL

**(We will also see further confirmation and elucidation from Santa Kumura in the chapter entitled, "Sanat Kumara Speaks".)**

# The End to this Eternal Story
*(Story Line - Gnosis)*

The Eternals who are truly the essence of all existence, have tended the garden of creation with love and great care, now walk entirely among us for this grand experiment is now winding down to its perfected completion. As these great teachers and ancient ones were there in the beginning they are now here at the end. For this is one of the main answers to the greatest riddle, *"the First will be the last and the Last will be the first,"* the First Begotten Being; Jesus and his Twin, Mary Magdalene and the Last Begotten Being; Sanat Kumara and his Twin Sophia. Another way this is seen portrayed is in the description of Santa Kumara, stating that he is the oldest of the oldest and the youngest of the youngest.

The short story version is as follows:

The Last were also the first to incarnate into the materially created form, with the imbuing of their first born; perfect divine human beings – Zoe and El Morya (as Eve and Seth). The infusion of the First Melchizedek to the planet was El Morya. The Egyptian Goddess Nephthys was the First Female to Ascend; she was the twin sister of Isis/Sophia. The first mystery school for Ascension was setup by El Morya. Moreover, the final return from the end of creation to the beginning will be with the return of Sanat Kumara and his Twin Flame Sophia leading the Ascension promenade of the 12 Divine Eternal Twinships with Jesus and his Twin Flame – LAST, with all of the Self-Chosen Ones following them into the LIGHT.

From what I can tell through my connection to the Eternal Truth, all the First Begotten Divine Twinships are gathering for the quickening of this great transformation. A great ceremony is planned, which will involve all those who wish to attend. I believe this grand gathering will take place at the Great Pyramid in Giza.

This event being of galactic unparalleled proportion, with the "Halls of Records" revealed and all the sacred wisdom spread out in full gnosis. The apex of the Great Pyramid back in its proper place, and the full function of its divine grace lit up fully before all our hearts and one wholistic face. With everything in its divine place, we await the vortex portals complete embrace and as the 12 Eternal Twins set the pace, the entire self-chosen great race ascends directly back to that high space. From the outside, in, that great Merkaba will take all who resonate with the love of the ONE, within and beyond, for it is the star gate that we all create. Perhaps this is just a good story's ending or just maybe the actual beginning of another great universe in the void of this vacant energetic space.

*(The previous short soul channeled information was writing in Feb 1998, 9 months before I would go to Egypt for the second time and experience a series of events that would very closely resemble the latter. This will be elaborated upon in the chapter entitled; "Opening the Way")*

> "For the End is where the Beginning is. Blessed is the person who stands at rest in the beginning. And that person will be acquainted with the end and will not taste death". ~ Gospel of Thomas (The great significance of this will become crystal clear as we open all the seals within these pages.)

# Lonely for Love
*(Story Line - Gnosis)*

Perhaps the greatest mystery of all allegorically concealed throughout the ages in many forms of sacred literature is that GOD/GODDESS is within us, and in some case spelt right out. I believe this is the quintessential lesson or experience for everyone. Complete comprehension of this fundamental premise begets gnosis, which secures eternal life. Through this knowing we obtain knowledge and through the understanding we gain wisdom, which is the truth that sets us free. The first saying recorded in the Gospel of Thomas says:

*Jesus said, "Who ever finds the meaning of these words will not taste death." And the second saying says, "Let the one who seeks not stop seeking until that person finds; and upon finding, that person will be astounded, and will reign over the entirety and gain repose."*

Before we can truly comprehend the answer to the question of the greatest mystery we must understand what the "Quest" or "Seeking" is truly all about. The age-old longing or searching can be found in many places through out history, to know Gods love, as well as the love of another. Simply to be loved. The desire and need of love is by far the most sought after experience, even out weighing the age-old lust of power and money. The individuals who sought the latter believed they could buy love or satiate the desire. I believe that quite possibly this is a primordial quest, originating with creation itself.

It is very plausible that it all began in the beginning with an experience or desire that was sought outside of self. There are several stories about how "God" (perhaps these stories are really about Yaldabaoth) creating Sabaoth, and all the extenuating Lords, galaxies and races, to know love or be loved. Yet he still was lonely and desired the company and love of another. Perhaps the quest has never changed, handed down through the ages as an inheritance of sorts. It would also seem that the result has never changed as well. One can never find complete love outside of self; if you are not complete within yourself and love yourself totally you will never be able to fully experience the love of another.

I believe this has almost become common knowledge, perhaps a golden rule. So perhaps through our growth and lessons "God" has also experienced love of self through Self. What I have come to know is that the basic principle of the mystery is to seek and know love of self as a love of GOD/GODDESS as one and the same.

I truly believe, with all my heart, that the main reason for the experience of separation, or perhaps better stated the illusion of a separation, was to realize through a process of complete self-analysis and discovery that we are not separate at all.

Perhaps in learning the lesson or gaining the experience the illusion of separation no longer serves. All is One and ONE IS ALL. To truly know self is to know GOD/GODDESS and to completely love self is to love GOD/GODDESS. The truth becomes GOD/GODDESS knows love of self through self as Self: "US", you and me. What a Mystery! This is the message of the Melchizedeks, the Saviors, the Avatars and the Eternals, which are all one and the same.

I have this basic tenant of truth in my heart of hearts since I was in my teens. It was truly wonderful to find this understanding reflected in the Gnostic Scriptures.

*Jesus says' "Tell me, if a person does not know how to love God, how will he be able to love himself? And how will he be able to love others if he is not able to love himself? I tell you the truth, that whoever has found a true friend has found one of the delights of Paradise - No! More than that - for such a one is a key to Paradise." ~ Gospel of Barnabas*

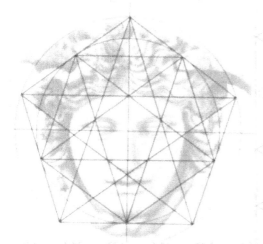

# Three Key principles for the Dimensional Shift
*(Story Line - Gnosis)*

The most important principles to assure that you will vibrate to the frequency of the 5th dimension and become an ascended being follows in the next three chapters.

## UNCONDITIONAL LOVE

A completely open heart of unconditional love requires an acceptance of self and a willingness to be in harmony between the masculine and feminine aspects of your being. Unconditional self-love and self-acceptance embraces all that we are. Honoring and recognizing your path of awakening and self-discovery with unconditional love gives you the awareness and understanding that you are in a state of perfect becoming. You are completely the sum total of your experiences, which have been the sculptures tool of molding your self-expression.

Unconditional love allows you the natural divine flow to unfold into the perfect being you are, trusting your process of soul evolution on your journey home. Unconditional love of self is the direct reflection of unconditional love of others; as you love your self unconditionally with divine compassion the Christ Consciousness within truly sees the reflection of self in all beings. Thus *unconditional love* is the natural uninhibited innate state of pure utter GOD LOVE, for we are GOD/GODDESS, the divine perfect human being, the twin DAUGHTER/SON Creators of this experience; a physical expression in matter.

## HEALTHY INNER CHILD

An open healthy relationship with your inner child aspect is also of paramount importance. A description and definition of the inner child will be helpful in your perception of the process of becoming whole. The inner child is akin to our emotions or emotional body, for the emotional body is much like a child. It does not understand reason or logic. Like a child, it views the material world with an innocent heart and eyes. A child's only wish is to be loved and accepted unconditionally for who they are as a being of pure light. A child's emotional body is easily hurt and misunderstood, often seeking fortitude deeply layered beneath its past experiences, this life and others, as well as; the great wall of pain, as a front, or barrier that has been set up to protect and conceal the deeper sensitivities.

This wall is commonly known as the over active or blown ego, the mechanism of self-defense and survival. So the inner child metaphorically speaking is our suppressed or hidden emotions. When the Master Jesus said, *be like little children, then you will enter the Kingdom of Heaven.*" Moreover, simply stated, aligning with the soul, which is ultimately innocent, we become filled with our child like nature, whose only wish is to learn more about love and experience it. This is the awe of child-like wonder. This is what Jesus was talking about.

It is paramount to this work to recognize the correlation of the feminine qualities with the emotional body, which are the exact opposite to the mental body or male aspect. The clearing and releasing of issues rooted in and blocking the open expression of the emotional body is probably the single most important factor in becoming a balanced, open hearted, self realized being, unconditionally loving and enlightened being.

RELATIONSHIP WITH MOTHER EARTH

An open healthy relationship with Mother Earth is also very important; she is in this process of transform as well and can assist you in many ways. It is very critical that you really come to love life and the planet; this is all part of learning to completely love the process. Actually, connecting to the Logos of Mother Earth, the Spirit of the Goddess and the Universal Creative force, the Mother of all, which strengths the connection to our emotional body. She is very real and can help you heal many things.

I cannot over emphasize the importance of grounding, connecting to the Earth. You need to be in your body fully to really feel your emotions and release issues. So many beings lose sight of this and when the going gets tough become ungrounded as a means to escape dealing with the clearing of difficult issues. In other words, jumping out of the body or going into the astral plane so one does not need to feel the pain.

*The Five initiations and axioms, which were referred to in the preface, have their direct correlation here, as the initiations of the Elements, the alchemical amalgamation of the four base elements into the fifth Etheric. The first two are specific to the keys above and those in the following chapter.*

*Initiation by Water (Baptism by Water) – clears the emotional body. One must release any blocks within the heart or the emotional body in order to truly begin to under go the greater transformations. Here we find a greater understanding of the First Initiation. This involves removing emotional blocks, which enable the heart to be filled with divine love. This is the exalted emotion that enables being fully present in the now moment. The place where we can truly feel absolutely free and completely fulfilled. From this space the divine flow of synchronicity is accessed effortlessly. This also enables the depth of passion and desire necessary to realize your greatest potential. This is the first of two fundamental elements, that when equally balanced, are the fundamental ingredients required for manifesting on this plane.*

*Initiation by Air (Baptism by Fire) – This goes hand in hand with the first step. However, it deals with the release of all programming or out dated belief systems that are hindering the mental body from fully aligning to and accessing the oversoul. Fire is actually light or better understood as the higher and finer frequencies of divine consciousness. This is quintessential to changing ones reality, for our beliefs are held in place by our mental constructs. This material is designed to help one realize that they are the masters of their reality. In order to change the reality that is experienced one must change their mind.*

*These two elements (Water and Fire, i.e. Heart and Mind) represent one half of the equation represented by the Merkaba.*

# Seven powerful keys to the "Inner Door"
### (Story Line - Gnosis)

The following is a very good process for releasing issues that can arise from awakening to truth.

## 1.    Recognition

Admit to your self when your issues are surfacing, recognizing when your buttons are being pushed. Have the courage to allow your ego and defenses to come down long enough to fully perceive what is happening.

## 2.    Acceptance

The complete acknowledgment that this is your issue, your reaction to an action is required. Take full ownership of the issue, without rationalizing it away as outside of yourself or as a projection onto you or blaming others. Basically accepting the responsibility of facing your fears and inner shadowed secrets. Your are half way there to releasing them now. Acceptance is bringing them into the light to be transformed.

## 3.    Realization

This is the understanding that your issue is a lesson set up for you by yourself for your own growth. That the person who is causing your issue to come to the surface is actually a compassionate being that you contracted with to play the "Bad Guy" so you could see your own stuff more clearly.

## 4.    Release

The actual healing occurs from having the intention and determination of moving through the issue. The most strength and courage was required in the previous steps. Just by facing the issue and having the desire from the heart to move through it, the issue is removed almost by divine intervention. Taking a look at the root or core of your beliefs often helps you understand why you felt or reacted the way you did. Having embraced it in the light of truth, it is dissolved. The process may need to be repeated according to various aspects or angels of the core issue. The "Truth" is, you are a spiritual being, having a human experience and you are not actually your experiences, but a divine being on the highest path to enlightenment and greater world service. In this truth, you gain the knowledge and understanding of the experiences and how they relate to your path.

5. Gratification

Giving thanks for the gift by thanking the messenger for delivering the gift. Thanking the human being for playing the "Bad Guy" openly or inwardly is full release. This individual may be someone in passing, an acquaintance, or an actual significant other in your life, as relationships often are the greatest opportunity for growth.

6. Forgiveness and Compassion

Respect and honor all aspects of the experience. Have compassion towards anyone who has been involved, including yourself. Know that everything is perfect and in accordance with Divine Will. Be thankful, forgive all and trust your self and your process.

7. **Love Yourself!**

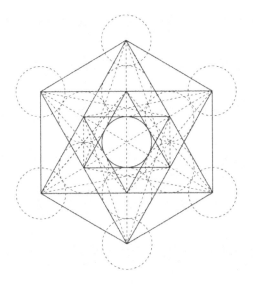

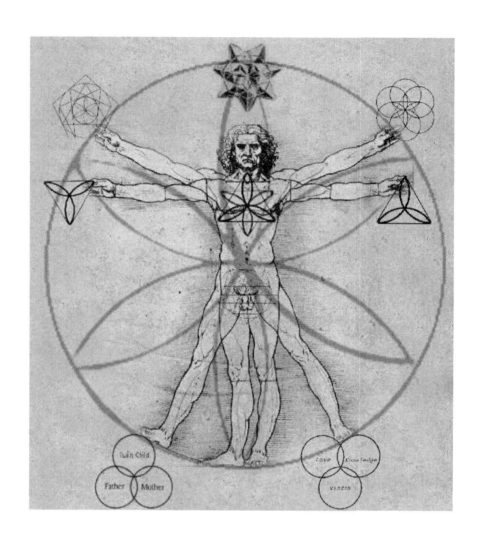

# The Energy Retrieval Process *(Story Line - Gnosis)*

## I    Identify Patterns

Open to Awareness by stepping back from the everyday focus on reality. Identify patterns in your life that are repeating in ways that do not support your fullest Divine expression of Love, Happiness and Joy. (If emotions are already triggered, skip this step.)

## II    Establish Connection

The pattern carries a message/reflection, which is revealed in a mirror that holds charge for you. Place awareness on the message /reflection or part of self that is feeling unloved. Go into feelings and embrace the fragmented part of self which has been causing disharmony in your life; it is the source of the charge or energy that gets triggered to show you unresolved judgments or childhood decisions.

**Three things may occur here.**
a) Charge may release automatically; process complete.
b) Charge may just completely shut you down or freeze you up. (That's ok; start moving the energy by walking, bodywork or have someone rock your inner child. The process will be re-triggered as emotions surface, allowing process to completion.)
c) Charge may really bring up strong emotions; go to next step.

## III    Engage Emotions

Allow the moving of all emotions necessary to experience the source of the original charge. Really listen to the reflection's message and hear its discomfort with separation from true self (you). Getting in touch with that part and communicating with it is actually loving yourself whole. Open completely to understanding what the reflection is trying to tell you. Identifying with the underlying decision or issue fully releases the charge.

## IV    Release

Nurture and comfort self from a deep understanding heart space. Love this lost/found part of your self as a gift. Welcome any further pieces surrounding this reflection and just be with it in your new awareness.

## V    Integration

Reprogram integrated aspect with a healthy, balanced affirmation. Full integration may take a moment, hours or weeks. Welcome any revisiting of the issue during integration process.

Use these tools to become the full expression of your Divine Self in the now moment.

## Matrix of Polarities
*(Story Line - Gnosis)*

| | | |
|---|---|---|
| Evil | - | Good |
| Soul | - | Spirit |
| Thought | - | Emotions |
| Mind | - | Feelings |
| Positive | - | Negative |
| Electricity | - | Magnetism |
| Psyche | - | Intuitive |
| Aggressive | - | Passive |
| Separation | - | Unity |
| Ego | - | Compassion |
| Form | - | Formless |
| Air | - | Earth |
| Fire | - | Water |
| Light | - | Dark |
| Knowledge | - | Love |
| Even | - | Odd |
| Right | - | Left |
| Limited | - | Unlimited |
| Male | - | Female |
| Active | - | Receptive |

WHITE

BLACK

One cannot exist without the other.
For if white did not exist, you would not
know that black was there, for all would
be dark. White reveals black, and dark
reveals Light. Without each other no one
would experience a single day or night.

The table of opposites essentially helps one to see the mental construct that have been twisted to limit or confine the Spirit of Humanity into belief systems designed to create dis-empowerment of the I AM Self.

Here we find a greater understanding of the expansion of the mental body (baptism by fire), removing blocks that limit the potential for the I AM PRESENCE to fully create realities as an unadulterated divine expression of the will of the ONE. The full manifestation of the out picturing of self as SELF is simply not possible if you do not believe it to be so. This also enables the clarity of the highest of intentions to become the second element or tool of manifestation. The entire extant of this written material is designed to expand your awareness to divine proportions.

See the reflection and know the truth of unity as ONE!

# Afterword

At this point we have completed a general frame work of understanding that sets the stage for erecting our temple of the greater mysteries. The lesser mysteries touched on all the fundamental components necessary to prepare you for the whole story. Now we will elaborate on the highlights required for Divine Gnosis.

In order to shift the perspective for an expanded view or new mental construct, we must first acquaint you with the difference between text book history, the views of politically constrained Egyptology, verses the unfettered approach of a spiritually freed truth seeker. Who is only interested in the greater good of the whole.

The recounting of the past through the lens of the oversoul of the author constitutes the neo-history necessary to connect the golden threads through the greater tapestry of our Divine Heritage.

The evidence of the existence of beings with higher intelligence and higher consciousness becomes overwhelming as we begin to look at the underlying meaning of various myths, folklore, ancient scripts and stone configurations.

The collaboration between obscure keys within the previous subjects are the backbone that will support the self-evident truth that an ancient advanced scientific, spiritual and meta-physical civilization was not only existent, but is prophesied to return as the Golden Age draws ever near in our lives.

**[This journey of self discovery is a bit like peeling an onion, there are so many layers to who we are, have been and are in the multiverse. The ancient wisdom is literally volumes of material. My journey to find the things that I innately knew has consumed nearly every waking moment of my entire life. The urging by my guides and higher self to uncover certain truths that tell a greater story has been some times relentless. I have been astonished many times by things that I was guided to look deeper into or behind. I have assembled all this in the body of work that is overall entitled Gnosis Unveiled. You can find videos that elaborate on all the aspects of this material on youtube under Mathues Imhotep. Enjoy the Journey!]**

**Final after thoughts. From where I am now in my consciousness and journey I know so much more than I did all those years ago. I know there is a language of light, a pristine source code and a divine operating system (DOS…lol). In the next volume we will start to decode the original angel language that is use to create reality.**

**We will learn why this type of symbolism is so important and what it was hiding in the next volume.**

Made in the USA
Coppell, TX
14 January 2021